Pandemics

by Debra A. Miller

LUCENT BOOKS

An imprint of Thomson Gale, a part of The Thomson Corporation

THOMSON

GALE

Detroit • New York • San Francisco • San Diego • New Haven, Conn. • Waterville, Maine • London • Munich

© 2007 Thomson Gale, a part of The Thomson Corporation.

Thomson and Star Logo are trademarks and Gale and Lucent Books are registered trademarks used herein under license.

For more information, contact:
Lucent Books
27500 Drake Rd.
Farmington Hills, MI 48331-3535
Or you can visit our Internet site at http://www.gale.com

LIBRARY OF CONGRESS CATALOGING-IN-PUBLICATION DATA

Miller, Debra A.
  Pandemics / Debra A. Miller.
    p. cm. — (Hot topics)
  Includes bibliographical references and index.
  ISBN 1-59018-965-5 (hard cover : alk. paper) 1. Communicable diseases—Juvenile literature. 2. Epidemics—Juvenile literature. I. Title. II. Series: Hot topics (San Diego, Calif.)
  RA643.M55 2006
  618.92'9—dc22
                                                          2006007057

Printed in the United States of America

CONTENTS

FOREWORD

Young people today are bombarded with information. Aside from traditional sources such as newspapers, television, and the radio, they are inundated with a nearly continuous stream of data from electronic media. They send and receive e-mails and instant messages, read and write online "blogs," participate in chat rooms and forums, and surf the Web for hours. This trend is likely to continue. As Patricia Senn Breivik, the dean of university libraries at Wayne State University in Detroit, states, "Information overload will only increase in the future. By 2020, for example, the available body of information is expected to double every 73 days! How will these students find the information they need in this coming tidal wave of information?"

Ironically, this overabundance of information can actually impede efforts to understand complex issues. Whether the topic is abortion, the death penalty, gay rights, or obesity, the deluge of fact and opinion that floods the print and electronic media is overwhelming. The news media report the results of polls and studies that contradict one another. Cable news shows, talk radio programs, and newspaper editorials promote narrow viewpoints and omit facts that challenge their own political biases. The World Wide Web is an electronic minefield where legitimate scholars compete with the postings of ordinary citizens who may or may not be well-informed or capable of reasoned argument. At times, strongly worded testimonials and opinion pieces both in print and electronic media are presented as factual accounts.

Conflicting quotes and statistics can confuse even the most diligent researchers. A good example of this is the question of whether or not the death penalty deters crime. For instance, one study found that murders decreased by nearly one-third when the death penalty was reinstated in New York in 1995.

Death penalty supporters cite this finding to support their argument that the existence of the death penalty deters criminals from committing murder. However, another study found that states without the death penalty have murder rates below the national average. This study is cited by opponents of capital punishment, who reject the claim that the death penalty deters murder. Students need context and clear, informed discussion if they are to think critically and make informed decisions.

The Hot Topics series is designed to help young people wade through the glut of fact, opinion, and rhetoric so that they can think critically about controversial issues. Only by reading and thinking critically will they be able to formulate a viewpoint that is not simply the parroted views of others. Each volume of the series focuses on one of today's most pressing social issues and provides a balanced overview of the topic. Carefully crafted narrative, fully documented primary and secondary source quotes, informative sidebars, and study questions all provide excellent starting points for research and discussion. Full-color photographs and charts enhance all volumes in the series. With its many useful features, the Hot Topics series is a valuable resource for young people struggling to understand the pressing issues of the modern era.

WHEN MICROORGANISMS ATTACK

Microorganisms, including viruses, bacteria, fungi, and protozoa, are tiny, simple, but extremely hardy and ancient life-forms that pose dangerous threats to the much more complex and newer human species. These simple organisms have almost always existed and probably always will. Some of the oldest fossils from billions of years ago are those of primitive bacteria, and they very likely constituted some of the earliest forms of life on earth. As higher life-forms developed, these tiny organisms went on the attack. Fossils of the earliest plants show fungus infections; the bones of dinosaurs, mastodons, and saber-toothed tigers show evidence of bacterial infections; and the remains of early humans reveal bone infections at the site of fractures, along with chronic infections such as tooth decay and arthritis. Microorganisms, also called "germs" or "microbes," are simply part of the food chain on Earth, in which all creatures feed upon other creatures and are, in turn, fed upon themselves.

The Process of Infection

When microorganisms meet humans, the first encounter often leads to infection, especially if the body is unfamiliar with that particular type of germ. The human body's immune system responds and in most cases wins the battle, killing off the invader germs with fever, chemicals, or attack cells called antibodies. In fact, illness among humans tends to be the exception rather than the rule, even though there are literally hundreds of thousands of species of potentially dangerous microbes living everywhere around us—in the soil, in water, and in virtually every type of creature that lives. Often, the body can even produce lifelong immunity against particular germs. Sometimes, too, the human defenses are good but not perfect and a type of standoff occurs, in which certain symptoms become chronic but are not lethal. In other cases, however, the end result may be death, for both the human host and the microbe.

Whatever the outcome, throughout this process of infection, rapidly multiplying germs or their descendants may reach new human hosts through sneezing, coughing, bleeding, diarrhea, or other means of transmission. Indeed, the most formidable weapon of microorganisms is their ability to replicate and modify themselves quickly, evolving in many different directions in a fight to survive. The microbes change their genes, or mutate, each time they reproduce, enabling them to adapt to

Germs travel through the air in droplets expelled by a sneeze. Diseases are also spread by coughing, bleeding, and diarrhea.

new environments easily and jump between animal, plant, and human species.

Periodically during this process, a completely new, extremely lethal microorganism is created—one that is able to spread rapidly from person to person and kill many of the humans it encounters. This rapid spread is called an epidemic. If the epidemic occurs over a wide geographic area, it is called a pandemic—a word derived from the Greek words *pan*, meaning "all," and *demos*, meaning "people."

A History of Pandemics

Experts say that early humans probably experienced their share of epidemic infections. Such outbreaks may have wiped out whole clans or tribes. These first epidemics could not spread far, however, because early humans lived in small, nomadic groups that were widely dispersed and isolated from each other, preventing germs from reaching too many people. Around ten thousand years ago, with the beginning of agriculture and the domestication of animals, humans began to settle down and form larger communities. With people living closer both to each other and to a variety of animals, microbes were able to gain a stronger foothold. This process has occurred throughout history; each time human civilization has undergone changes or affected environments in novel ways, it has created opportunities for new infectious microorganisms to arise.

In the last few centuries, as human populations have grown dramatically and human activities have expanded around the globe, infectious diseases have been able to spread across oceans and continents to kill millions of people—more than either wars or famine. In just five years in the mid-fourteenth century, for example, one-third of Europe's population died of the bubonic plague, a disease spread from Asia by Mongol armies, who inadvertently brought along rats carrying infected fleas. Later centuries saw wave after wave of infectious diseases, many of which spread through trade, exploration, or other travel throughout the world. The twentieth century brought the most deadly pandemic of all—the 1918 Spanish influenza, caused by a virus that killed tens of millions around the globe.

Infectious Disease Today

During most of these past disease pandemics, people had no idea what was causing the illnesses. Sickness was thought to be a punishment from God, or the result of gases from decaying matter (called "bad air"), or even the product of an unlucky alignment of the moon and stars. Modern scientists finally solved the mystery by showing that invisible microorganisms cause disease, and medical advancements soon slowed the tide of infectious disease with new vaccines and medicines.

Despite these successes, however, today infectious disease is once again on the rise. Acquired immunodeficiency syndrome, known as AIDS, a deadly new disease for which there is no cure, and two ancient diseases, tuberculosis and cholera, are now rampant in undeveloped countries, causing millions of deaths each year. Health authorities, too, are worried about avian flu, a

A young mother is one of millions of people around the world who suffers from tuberculosis.

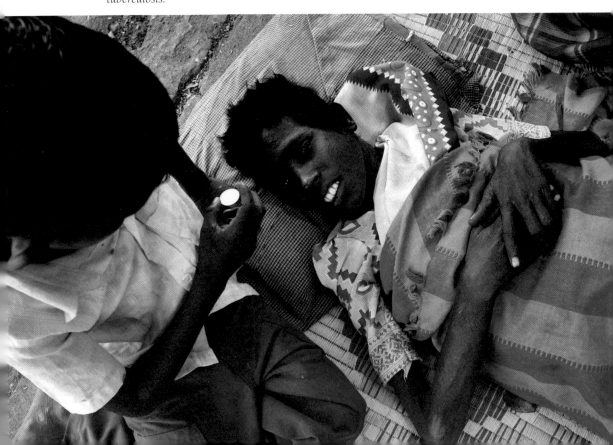

new influenza (or flu) threat, this time caused by a virus that appears to be evolving to humans from birds. In an age of globalization, when people and goods can carry germs rapidly around the world, any new deadly disease could be devastating for all countries. Also, human technology now enables diseases to be used as weapons, raising the specter of accidental or intentional release of lethal microbes that could spark a worldwide pandemic.

People in developed countries, such as the United States, often forget about the dangers of infectious disease because they have been protected since birth by vaccines, medicines, and clean food and water and may never have experienced serious illness. Earth's soaring population growth and increasing international travel and trade, however, provide fertile ground for the creation of new diseases from which no one will be safe. Only by applying human intelligence, through research, planning, and global cooperation, can humans hope to control infectious microorganisms.

THE THREAT FROM INFECTIOUS PANDEMICS

Throughout history, human activities, such as wars, trade, exploration, population growth, and urban crowding, have opened the door to new infectious diseases that have spread far and wide. These raging disease pandemics, and the deaths they caused, in turn, often altered the course of human history. Disease has affected the outcome of wars, upset the power of kings, helped to end dynasties, and led to the creation of new empires. As bacteriologist Hans Zinsser said, "Soldiers have rarely won wars. They more often mop up after the barrage of epidemics."[1] Scientific and medical advancements in the late 1800s and early 1900s finally helped to stem the ravages of many ancient diseases, but much of what we know as the modern world has been molded by these past pandemics.

The First Pandemics

The world's first known pandemic probably began in Ethiopia. It traveled to Egypt and Libya and then in 430 B.C. erupted in ancient Greece during the Peloponnesian war between Athens and Sparta. Greek historian Thucydides left a written record of the disease's frightening symptoms: "People in good health were all of a sudden attacked by violent heats in the head, and redness and inflammation in the eyes, the inward parts, such as the throat or tongue, becoming bloody and emitting an unnatural and fetid breath."[2] Next came sneezing, coughing, diarrhea, vomiting, and spasms, followed by the growth of pustules and ulcers on the skin and unquenchable thirst. Most people died by the seventh or eighth day. The few who survived were often left blind, missing fingers or toes, or with memory loss. The disease

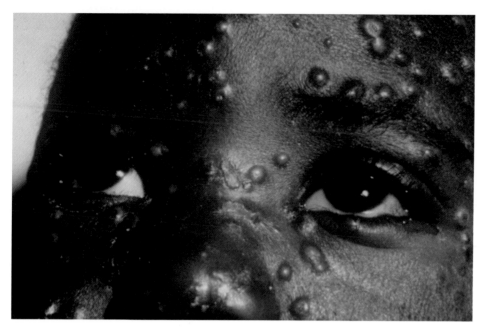

Painful sores are the principal symptom of smallpox, a devastating disease that has more than once reached epidemic proportions.

has never been diagnosed, but modern scientists suspect that it may have been smallpox. The outbreak killed about a third of the population of Athens, decimated its army, and helped to reduce the city's domination of Greece for a time.

Similar deadly diseases were instrumental in reducing the enormous power of the Roman Empire a few centuries later. The first outbreak struck Rome between A.D. 165 and 180, when Roman soldiers returning from eastern military campaigns brought home a new disease. The disease was called the plague of Antonius because it killed Marcus Aurelius Antonius, a Roman emperor, along with about 5 million other Romans. Like the plague that hit Greece, the Roman plague caused fever, throat inflammation, diarrhea, and skin lesions—symptoms typical of smallpox.

Between 255 and 266, a second disease outbreak with the same symptoms hit Rome. This later outbreak was just as deadly, at one point killing more than five thousand people each day. The toll taken by the two bouts of disease caused the Roman Empire to suspend its military crusades to other parts of the world and, many scholars believe, contributed significantly to its ultimate decline in power.

The Black Death

The most well-known pandemic in world history is today simply called "the plague." Although some scientists question its cause, experts have long believed that the illness was caused by bacteria that grow in infected fleas and are transferred to humans during flea bites. An early version of the plague came in two forms—the bubonic plague, which caused large tumors on the neck or in the armpits or groin, and the less common but even more virulent pneumonic plague, which attacked the respiratory system and caused people to cough up blood. A later version of the disease, septicemic plague, became known as the Black Death because it caused a hemorrhaging of blood under the skin that made the victims' skin look black. Once symptoms began, most victims died a miserable death within just a few days. As Italian writer Giovanni Boccaccio noted, victims sometimes "ate lunch with their friends and dinner with their ancestors."[3] The disease was also highly contagious: Anyone who came into contact with plague victims or even touched them or their belongings after death could also come down with the sickness.

PLAGUES AND CITIES

"Plagues and cities have always developed together."

Arno Karlen, science writer. Arno Karlen, *Man and Microbes*. New York: G.P. Putnam's Sons, 1995, p. 48.

The first wave of the illness, called the Plague of Justinian, hit Europe in A.D. 541, at its peak killing ten thousand people per day. A second outbreak in 588 spread the illness even farther. The plague then disappeared for about eight hundred years, but it returned with a vengeance in the middle of the fourteenth century. This time, it broke out in Asia and was spread by Mongol armies to Europe, probably by fleas living on rats that stowed away with the soldiers. Between 1346 and 1350, the plague killed almost a third of Europe's population—an estimated 25 million people. Outbreaks continued in Europe until the 1700s. Hardest hit were densely populated cities, where

Jesuit priests prepare the bodies of plague victims for burial in Spain in the sixteenth century.

many people lived in dirty conditions in which rats found an abundance of food and multiplied quickly, along with flea populations. The plague also spread across Africa, the Middle East, and Asia. By the time it ended, the disease had destroyed a third of Asia's and half of Europe's population. Over the centuries, the pandemic killed a staggering 137 million people worldwide.

The plague had an enormous impact on history. So many people died that a labor shortage developed in Europe, and peasants who survived the disease were able to demand higher wages. Many survivors simply took over the land of their dead neighbors, increasing their wealth almost overnight. With more income, peasants could afford medicine and better housing and living conditions, leading to improvements in hygiene and health. Buoyed by their newfound wealth and freedoms, peasants in Great Britain, France, and Italy began to rebel against unfair taxation and other repressive decrees ordered by their kings. The power of the Roman Catholic Church, too, began to decline because people lost their religious faith after being surrounded by so much death. These social upheavals paved the way for the Renaissance, a period in the fourteenth century in which art, architecture, literature, and learning blossomed in Europe. People's questioning of religion ultimately led in the sixteenth century to the Reformation, a movement that sought to reform the Roman Catholic Church and resulted in the establishment of a new Protestant branch of Christianity.

Exploration, Trade, Wars, and Disease

In the sixteenth and seventeenth centuries, when people began to travel and trade even more widely, exploring continents around the globe, waves of infectious disease often followed in their wake. European traders caught mosquito-borne diseases such as malaria and yellow fever in tropical Africa, India, Southeast Asia, and New Guinea. These diseases were soon spread to the New World of the Americas by European slave ships traveling from West Africa. Thousands of French soldiers sent by Napoleon to Haiti, for example, died from yellow fever. In fact, the risk of disease for French troops protecting New World possessions ultimately convinced Napoleon to sell the Louisiana

Territory to the United States in 1803. This fateful decision added more than 827,980 square miles (2,144,476 sq km) to U.S. lands—a region covering much of today's states of Louisiana, Arkansas, Missouri, Iowa, Minnesota, North Dakota, South Dakota, Nebraska, Kansas, Oklahoma, Texas, New Mexico, and parts of Montana, Wyoming, and Colorado.

Smallpox and another deadly disease, measles, also were introduced into the New World after killing many in Europe and Asia. Spanish conquistadors who had survived these diseases in Europe developed immunity, but when these explorers traveled to Central America, they infected vulnerable native populations who had never been exposed to these particular germs. Altogether, these two diseases killed much of the native population of the Americas—as many as 300 million people—and destroyed many of the native cultures. Toribio Motolinia, a Spanish priest, wrote that in most Aztec provinces, "more than half the population died . . . in heaps, like bedbugs. Many others died of starvation, because, as they were all taken sick at once, they could not care for each other."[4] Historians say infectious disease, rather than military might, was the main reason that Spain was able to conquer Mexico and large parts of Latin America and convert most of the region to Spain's Roman Catholic faith.

The next disease to become a true worldwide pandemic was cholera, caused by a bacterium that thrives in contaminated food and water and causes massive vomiting, diarrhea, dehydration, and rapid death. The disease is especially dangerous for children, who are extremely vulnerable to dehydration. India, where filthy water and poor living conditions are common, has historically suffered from this disease. Beginning about 1816, however, outbreaks occurred in other parts of the world, as seven separate waves of cholera rapidly spread along trade routes. The disease often took hold in the heavily populated cities that arose during the Industrial Revolution, where many people lived in squalid conditions with contaminated water sources. The first wave of disease reached as far as China, and the second pandemic, during the years 1829 to 1851, hit Europe, Canada, New York, and even America's Pacific coast. The third outbreak spread cholera to Russia, where it caused more than a million deaths. Later pandemics spread the illness to Africa and back again to Europe and Russia. The last pandemic began in Indonesia in 1961 and spread to Bangladesh, India, and Russia. Indeed, cholera has ravaged every continent in the world except Antarctica. Other bacterial diseases, such as tuberculosis and typhoid, also have spread around the world at various times throughout history.

NEW DISEASES

"Three causal elements in establishing a new disease within the human population appear to be traveling, starting to live in new environments, and living in close proximity to each other."

Pete Moore, science writer. Pete Moore, *Killer Germs: Rogue Diseases of the Twenty-First Century*. London: Carlton Books, 2001, p. 44.

Wars, too, produced disease epidemics that sometimes spread from country to country. One of the most prevalent wartime diseases was typhus, a bacterial illness that produces high fever and body rash and is transmitted to humans from lice or from fleas that thrive on animals such as squirrels or rats. Typhus spread rapidly in places where people lived in cramped quarters, such as war camps, jails, and ships. Typhus first emerged in the eleventh century during the Crusades, when it killed more men than were lost in battle. Another outbreak in 1528 killed eighteen thousand French troops fighting in Italy, causing France to lose dominance there to the Spanish. In 1542, thirty thousand people in the Balkans died of typhus while fighting the Ottomans. Centuries later, in 1811, typhus reportedly helped to destroy Napoleon's army in Russia, and during World War II it killed many prisoners in the Nazi concentration camps.

In the 1800s a new infectious and highly communicable viral disease—poliomyelitis, or polio—hit the developed world. Unlike many past pandemics, this disease primarily struck healthy children. It caused sudden paralysis and was sometimes so aggressive that victims could no longer breathe on their own and were forced to live in iron lungs, large metal tanks invented to

Franklin D. Roosevelt, Polio Victim

In 1921, polio struck Franklin D. Roosevelt, then a wealthy and well-known politician from New York. At age thirty-nine, after an active day sailing and swimming while on vacation, Roosevelt suddenly fell ill. Doctors diagnosed his condition as polio. From that point on, Roosevelt lived with severe pain and extensive paralysis of his legs. With the aid of heavy steel braces, he could stand, but he required the assistance of strong men to keep him from falling. In the years that followed, Roosevelt courageously fought to strengthen his muscles, traveling often to Warm Springs, Georgia, where he established the first polio rehabilitation program. Refusing to be limited by his disability, Roosevelt reentered politics, and in 1932, he was elected president of the United States —an office he held until his death in 1945. Throughout his presidency, Roosevelt hid the full extent of his disability from the public by not allowing photographs showing him in a wheelchair and arranging appearances so that he was either seated or standing with support. Roosevelt is remembered as a great president, and he used his power to lead the fight against polio and make its cure a national goal.

A photograph shows a rare view of President Roosevelt in his wheelchair.

assist with respiration. Many victims died, and those who survived were often left with mild to severe paralysis, typically crippled legs and bodies. Large outbreaks of polio were recorded in Europe during the second half of the nineteenth century, and polio hit the eastern United States in 1894. By 1916, polio had become an epidemic in America, with over nine thousand cases in New York City alone. The disease even struck Franklin D. Roosevelt, who later became famous not only as a U.S. president but also for courageously battling the heartbreaking disease.

Spanish Flu—The Worst Pandemic in Recent History

The worst pandemic in recent history, however, was the Spanish influenza, which killed between 40 and 50 million people worldwide between 1918 and 1919—even more fatalities than were caused in the four worst years of the infamous Black Death. Incredibly, a quarter of all Americans caught the disease, along with a fifth of the population of the entire world. Now believed to have originated in China or the United States, the

Workers care for U.S. soldiers stricken with Spanish flu during World War I.

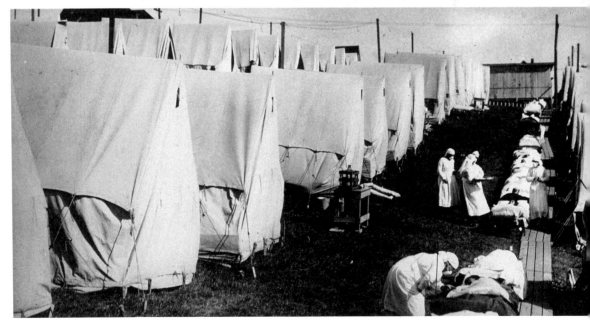

flu pandemic acquired its name when Spain became the first country to report a serious outbreak. Quickly, however, it spread around the globe—to North America, Europe, Asia, Africa, Brazil, and the South Pacific. Soldiers fighting in World War I were particularly affected, and in fact, half of all American soldiers who died during the war were killed not by the enemy, but by the Spanish flu.

The disease was unique because unlike most flus, which primarily hit children and the elderly, this flu was most deadly for people in the prime of life, ages twenty to forty. The disease was so lethal that some people woke up healthy, came down with the illness, and were dead by nightfall. A physician at the time wrote that patients would suddenly develop a terrible type of pneumonia and then "simply struggle for air until they suffocate."[5]

Despite the advances in medical knowledge and living conditions since the Middle Ages, the 1918 flu pandemic created

A Spanish Flu Story

On September 29, 1918, a doctor stationed at Camp Devens, a military base just west of Boston, wrote a letter to a friend, describing the effects of the Spanish flu. The letter, in part, stated:

This epidemic started about four weeks ago, and has developed so rapidly that the camp is demoralized and all ordinary work is held up till it has passed. . . . These men start with what appears to be an attack of la grippe or influenza, and when brought to the hospital they very rapidly develop the most vis-

cous type of pneumonia that has ever been seen. Two hours after admission they have the mahogany spots over the cheek bones, and a few hours later you can begin to see the cyanosis [a bluish discoloration of the skin] extending from their ears and spreading all over the face, until it is hard to distinguish the coloured men from the white. It is only a matter of a few hours then until death comes.

Quoted in PBS, "A Letter from Camp Devens, Massachusetts," September 29, 1918. www.pbs.org/wgbh/amex/influenza /sfeature/devens.html.

conditions similar to those during the Black Death. With so many people falling sick and dying, people became afraid to go out in public. The U.S. government shut down many public places, such as schools, churches, bars, and theaters, to prevent the transmission of the virus. The economy slowed, few people traveled, and funerals were held almost constantly. Hospitals, health care workers, medicines, and grave diggers soon were in short supply, and bodies piled up at morgues and, in some places, on the streets. Many people were buried quickly in mass graves. Other flu pandemics have occurred since the time of the Spanish flu—including the Asian flu in 1957 and the Hong Kong flu in 1968—but none has been anywhere near as deadly.

Science Success Stories

The 1918 flu's virulence spurred scientific and medical research on infectious diseases—a process that was already well under way. In the late nineteenth and early twentieth centuries, physicians and scientists began to understand the causes of many of the world's infectious diseases and sought to develop therapies or vaccines to cure or prevent them. As early as the 1600s, microscopes were available and amateur scientists recorded seeing small organisms in pond water and other places. Beginning in the late 1870s, scientists finally began to document that many infectious diseases are caused by these microorganisms, which are invisible to the human eye.

The father of this new field of microbiology was Louis Pasteur, a French chemist. Pasteur became famous in 1859 by debunking the theory of "spontaneous generation," which held that life (such as maggots) forms spontaneously from nonliving matter (such as rotting meat). Pasteur went on to prove that microscopic organisms live in the air, earth, and water—an idea known as "germ theory"—the basic principle behind the field of microbiology. Pasteur also discovered that boiling liquids can kill harmful microbes, a process that became known as "pasteurization." He helped found the modern science of immunology by discovering that he could save chickens from a type of chicken cholera by injecting them with an artificially created, weakened version of the cholera bacteria—in this way immunizing them against the disease. Using this process, Pasteur produced one of the world's first vaccines. It protected cattle against infections caused by a bacterium called anthrax.

Pasteur, however, was only building on the work of an earlier amateur scientist, Edward Jenner, an English country doctor who is credited with inventing the first vaccine for smallpox. At a time when smallpox was rampant in Europe, Jenner noted that milkmaids seemed to be immune to the disease. He theorized that the immunity came from cowpox, a mild disease similar to smallpox that causes blisters in humans, and that these blisters somehow inoculated the milkmaids against the much more seri-

Research by scientist Louis Pasteur gave the world a new understanding of germs and led to development of an anthrax vaccine for cattle.

ous human smallpox. In 1796, Jenner proved his theory by injecting the pus from a cowpox blister into a young boy. When he then injected the boy with human smallpox, the boy became ill but recovered within just a few days and was then immune to smallpox. At first, Jenner's claims were discounted, but by 1840 his treatment was used exclusively as the way to treat smallpox.

Along with Pasteur and Jenner, another towering figure in early microbiology was Robert Koch, a German doctor who became obsessed with finding microbes that cause human diseases. In 1878, Koch identified the germ that causes blood poisoning: He injected human tissue samples with a dye so that the organism could be more easily seen through a microscope. He also developed the procedures for proving that a particular microbe causes a particular disease—a process that involves isolating the microbe, growing it in a lab culture, and infecting a healthy host with the lab culture. Eventually, using another dye technique, Koch found the germs that cause tuberculosis and cholera.

The work of Koch, Pasteur, and Jenner inspired a generation of scientists dedicated to finding microorganisms that cause infectious disease. By the early 1900s, most scientists agreed that microorganisms, spread by human contact, insects, and food and water contamination, caused most of the known infectious diseases. These discoveries led governments in Europe and North America to construct municipal water mains, modern sewers, and water purification systems. Many developed countries also created and funded agencies to monitor disease; impose quarantines; inspect food; control rodents; and promote sanitation, personal hygiene, and public health. Because of these efforts, many pandemic diseases were eliminated from the developed areas of the world.

New Medical Advances

In the twentieth century, scientific knowledge expanded even further to develop ways to cure or prevent many types of infectious disease. Paul Ehrlich, an assistant in Koch's lab, laid the foundation for the modern field of antibiotics, medicines that are used to treat bacterial disease. Like Koch, Ehrlich used dyes to search out harmful microscopic organisms. He reasoned that if the dyes

Dr. Alexander Fleming discovered a germ-killing fungus (inset) which was later developed into a new drug called penicillin.

could be used to bind to one type of cell and not another, then perhaps chemicals could be developed to kill only the harmful microbes and not the surrounding tissues. Ehrlich began to search for a cure for syphilis, a sexually transmitted disease that was widespread in the late nineteenth century. In 1910, Erhlich found such a cure—a chemical compound he called salvarsan—that killed the syphilis infection but not the human hosts.

Later, other scientists developed antibiotics to cure a number of the world's other serious bacterial infections. In 1928, for example, Scottish doctor Alexander Fleming discovered a curious mold in his lab that could kill germs without affecting humans. Fleming's mold was developed in the 1940s by Howard Florey and Ernst Chain into an antibiotic medicine called penicillin —a miracle drug that cures various bacterial infections. Penicillin was a godsend during World War II, when it was used to treat infected wounds, historically the biggest wartime killer. Along with penicillin came the invention of sulfa drugs, synthetic chemical agents that also act against harmful microorganisms that cause bacterial infections. In the 1960s, still more antibiotics were developed for curing other infectious diseases, including tuberculosis, typhoid fever, and bubonic plague.

Antibiotics, however, worked only on diseases caused by bacterial microbes. Other research was necessary to find ways to control diseases caused by another type of microorganism called viruses. This branch of medicine blossomed in the 1950s, when Jonas Salk, a scientist at the University of Pittsburgh, developed the first vaccine for polio, helping to wipe out the disease in the Americas. Vaccines were later developed for other childhood viral diseases such as measles, rubella, and mumps, as well as for many modern varieties of influenza.

Eliminating Ancient Diseases

These successes against leading infectious diseases eliminated many of the ancient diseases in most parts of the world. Worldwide childhood vaccination programs, for example, completely eradicated smallpox, one of the most feared infectious diseases. On May 8, 1980, the World Health Assembly, a global health organization, formally declared, "The world and all its peoples have won freedom from smallpox."[6] Indeed, the remarkable achievements of modern medicine caused many scientists to predict that most infectious diseases would be permanently wiped out around the globe. In 1967, for example, U.S. surgeon general William H. Stewart was so hopeful about humans' ability to cope with infectious disease pandemics that he suggested it was "time to close the book on infectious diseases, declare the war against pestilence won, and shift national resources to such chronic problems as cancer and heart disease."[7] Stewart's optimism soon proved to be unfounded, however, as infectious disease began making a strong comeback.

CHAPTER 2

THE BATTLE AGAINST INFECTIOUS DISEASE CONTINUES

The dream of a world without disease was dashed in the 1970s, 1980s, and 1990s when old diseases resurfaced, some diseases became resistant to antibiotic drugs, and completely new diseases emerged. Even in the United States, deaths from infectious disease have doubled from what they were just decades ago, and in many less developed countries, infectious diseases have once again become a leading cause of death. Worldwide, infectious diseases are responsible for more than 13 million deaths each year. Scientists now believe that infectious diseases will continually emerge as microorganisms adapt; as the world's temperatures, food supplies, and habitats constantly change; and as human societies become ever more populated, complex, and global. Many experts today are even predicting that we may be entering a dangerous new era of infectious disease pandemics.

Globalization

Many factors are contributing to this growth of infectious diseases. The most important factor is globalization—changes in communication, transportation, and trade that make the nations of the world much more connected and interdependent than in past centuries. One of the most significant aspects of globalization, for example, is a huge increase in the numbers of people traveling internationally. According to statistics, the number of international airline passengers has increased sevenfold in the last fifty years, from 200 million in 1950 to a record 4 billion in 2005. This ability to travel easily is of great benefit to many people, but disease experts say it allows infectious diseases to be spread from country to country much more quickly than in the past. Today, by the time a disease outbreak is discovered, the chances are good that it already has been spread to other regions around the globe.

Globalization also has caused changes in food production that are bringing more disease into people's lives. Many food products are now grown or manufactured in large quantities, so that when contamination occurs, it is likely to affect many people.

Crowded cities and international air travel are two reasons why pathogens spread more swiftly than they ever have in the past.

Beef and chicken, for example, are today produced in factory farms owned by large multinational agribusiness companies. In these operations, tens of thousands of animals are raised in crowded, unsanitary conditions, and their carcasses are then processed quickly on mass production lines. If these jobs are not performed carefully, animal wastes containing dangerous microbes can easily infect the raw meat, and if the meat is then not cooked properly, or if it touches other foods before it is cooked, it can make people sick. Animal wastes can also easily infect produce if contaminated water is used for cleaning or irrigating fruits and vegetables.

CROSSING PATHS

"As modern life grows increasingly complex, humans and pathogens will more and more cross paths."

Madeline Drexler, science and medical journalist. Madeline Drexler, *Secret Agents: The Menace of Emerging Infections*. Washington, DC: Joseph Henry, 2002, p. 275.

Global trade of these food products only widens the reach of infectious disease. Multinational food companies produce, buy, and sell tons of meat, vegetable, and fruit products, so just one tiny bit of contamination can spread disease far and wide. Grocery stores today stock fresh fruits and vegetables from countries around the world, some of which may not have sanitary standards, increasing the chances for food contamination. Dr. Keith P. Klugman, a professor of health and medicine at Georgia's Emory University, explains, "While microbial evolution will continue, and new organisms and new threats will emerge, it's the potential for dissemination that has changed and that will pose the greatest threat to people in the next 100 years."[8]

Population and Environmental Changes

In addition to becoming more mobile, the world's human population today is rapidly expanding, increasing the numbers of people who live close together in cities and urban areas. This growth of densely populated cities, especially in developing countries

Germs easily breed and circulate in unsanitary living conditions like those found in this slum in Mumbai, India.

where unsafe water, unsanitary living conditions, and widespread poverty are rampant, creates fertile breeding grounds for disease. When diseases do break out, the crowded conditions enable infections to spread to many people in a short time.

In many areas of the world, too, human settlements are moving into previously wild regions, displacing animal habitats and exposing people and domestic animals to new microbes that can cause human disease. Often, domesticated animals such as pigs or chickens will acquire a disease first from contact with wild animals, and then the disease jumps from these farm animals to their human caretakers. In fact, according to Dr. David Suzuki, a Canadian scientist, "In the past 30 years, more than 35 new infectious diseases have been diagnosed. . . . And three quarters of all these emerging diseases have jumped from animals to humans."[9]

Other changes in the environment caused by humans also may be affecting levels of disease. Global warming, for example, appears to be causing changes in climates such as warmer air and water temperatures, and researchers suspect that these changes in some regions may be improving conditions for the growth of insects that act as carriers of infectious disease. Insect carriers such as mosquitoes are also developing resistance to chemicals developed to control them. As a result, mosquito populations have soared, threatening once again to spread ancient mosquito-borne diseases such as malaria and typhus. Today, as many as 3 million people die from mosquito-related illnesses each year.

Problems with Medicines

Yet another reason behind the increase in infectious disease today is the failure to use the vaccines or medicines that effectively controlled many diseases in the twentieth century. In some industrialized countries, people have become so lax about vaccinating their children against old diseases that these illnesses are reappearing. In poorer countries, infectious diseases are making an even bigger comeback because people and their governments cannot afford proper nutrition, sanitation, vaccination programs, or curative drugs and antibiotics. In the developing world, infectious diseases now account for half of all deaths and are the biggest killer of children and young adults.

A significant problem, too, is that many microorganisms that cause disease are adapting and developing resistance to many of the known antibiotics and drugs developed to fight infectious disease. Over the last few decades, numerous types of bacteria have become resistant to penicillin, one of the safest and most reliable antibiotic drugs. Doctors have coped by switching to other types of antibiotics, but today many diseases, including tuberculosis, gonorrhea, malaria, and childhood ear infections, have become resistant to a growing number of antibiotic drugs. Some strains of bacteria have even been discovered that are resistant to all known antibiotic drugs. Nobel laureate Joshua Lederberg warns, "We're running out of bullets for dealing with a number of these infections. . . . Patients are dying because we no longer in many cases have antibiotics that work."[10]

Experts say that resistance to antibiotics is inevitable over time, because while antibiotics kill most bacteria, there will always

Infection and Chronic Disease

Researchers have discovered that many chronic diseases, once considered to be caused by genetics, lifestyle, or environmental factors, may also be caused or worsened by infectious microorganisms. The breakthrough came in the 1980s when researchers found that intestine and stomach ulcers are caused by *Helicobacter pylori* bacteria; most ulcers can now be completely cured with antibiotics. Since then, the list of infection-caused chronic diseases is growing. Chronic liver disease, chronic lung disease, and certain kinds of cancers, such as stomach cancer, cervical cancer, liver cancer, and lymphomas, have also now been linked with some form of bacteria or virus. Scientists have even found evidence that a bacterium called *Chlamydia pneumoniae* can increase the risk of developing heart disease. Researchers are now looking for linkages between infections and other debilitating chronic diseases, such as asthma, Alzheimer's, and schizophrenia. In the future, many chronic diseases may be prevented by vaccines, treated with antibiotics, or otherwise controlled by avoiding infectious microbes.

Heliobacter pylori *bacteria (which appear as orange strands in this image) attach to a stomach lining.*

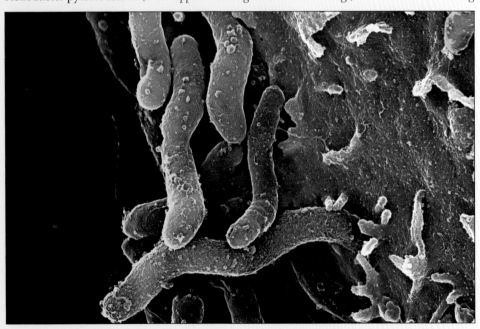

ANTIBIOTIC RESISTANCE

"Antibiotic resistance is something that directly affects everybody in this country, in a way that no single disease does."

J. Glenn Morris Jr., chairman of the Department of Epidemiology and Preventive Medicine at the University of Maryland School of Medicine. Quoted in Madeline Drexler, *Secret Agents: The Menace of Emerging Infections*. Washington, DC: Joseph Henry, 2002, p. 282.

be a resistant variant that is left alive, and this variant will then multiply and create a new generation of stronger, antibiotic-resistant microbes. Many in the field of microbiology believe, however, that this natural process of evolution has been speeded up by the overprescription of antibiotic drugs by doctors. Michael Blum, a medical officer with the U.S. Food and Drug Administration, explains, "Many [patients] have an expectation that when they're ill, antibiotics are the answer. They put pressure on the physician to prescribe them. Most of the time the illness is viral, and antibiotics are not the answer. This large burden of antibiotics is certainly selecting resistant bacteria."[11] Patients, too, sometimes fail to take antibiotic medicine for the full time prescribed by their physicians; this can also help to produce resistant bacteria. Another problem is the widespread use of antibiotics in agriculture, a practice in which healthy animals are given low levels of antibiotics to prevent diseases that might decrease the animals' weight gain and therefore their ultimate value. When the meat is then sold for human consumption, it may contribute to the growth of resistant bacteria in humans. All these factors have contributed to a host of old and new infectious threats.

AIDS/HIV—A New Disease Threat

One of the most challenging infectious diseases to arise in recent decades is a completely new type of virus called the human immunodeficiency virus (HIV), which causes a disease called acquired immunodeficiency syndrome, or AIDS. AIDS first came to the attention of the medical community in 1981, when an article in a scholarly medical magazine, the *New England Journal of*

Medicine, described the cases of four homosexual men who developed a host of serious infections due to a problem with their immune systems. Within a few years, researchers identified the virus that causes the immune system disease. No one knows for certain where the HIV virus came from, but many experts believe that the source was a virus in primates such as monkeys or apes that crossed the species dividing line to infect humans.

AIDS is spread by sexual contact or contact with infected blood. AIDS first struck the homosexual community, prostitutes, and intravenous drug users who used dirty needles for drug injections. Soon, however, AIDS moved into mainstream U.S. culture, infecting hundreds of thousands of heterosexual and drug-free people. Today, AIDS is spreading around the world, infecting millions.

Some people manage to live for ten or fifteen years with the AIDS virus, but many of those infected either die quickly or are

Chinese clinicians sort through AIDS/HIV medications. HIV infection rates are rapidly rising in China, as they are worldwide.

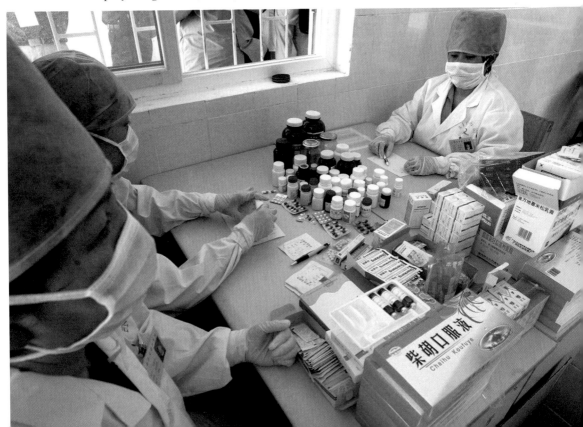

seriously ill for years while waiting to die. There is no known cure and no vaccine to prevent the disease, and no one has ever outlived the virus. A variety of drugs have been tested and found to slow the progression of AIDS, however. One of the most effective of these has been azidothymidine, or AZT. New drugs called HIV protease inhibitors offered great hope in recent years for defeating the HIV virus, but the effectiveness of these drugs appears to wear off after a time because the virus is so adaptable. Like the dreaded plague of the fourteenth century, AIDS so far appears unstoppable.

Tuberculosis and Malaria—Ancient Diseases Return

Much of the developing world is also being ravaged today by two diseases once thought to be under control—tuberculosis (TB) and malaria. TB is contracted by breathing in a tiny amount of a bacterium called *Mycobacterium tuberculosis*, which, if left untreated, gradually destroys the lungs, leading to death. Victims become short of breath and suffer from coughing, sneezing, fever, lack of energy, and weight loss. The process can take years and, in the late stages of the disease, victims become highly contagious. The English writer Charles Dickens provided one of the best descriptions of the disease: "There is a dread disease which so prepares its victims . . . for death . . . , in which the struggle between soul and body is so gradual, quiet, and solemn, and the result so sure, that day by day, and grain by grain, the mortal part wastes and withers away, so that the spirit grows light."[12]

In 1921, two French bacteriologists, Léon Charles Albert Calmette and Camille Guerin, invented the first viable vaccine for TB. The first antibiotic cure for TB was developed in 1943 by American microbiologist Selman A. Waksman, and a number of other anti-TB drugs appeared in the following years. Tuberculosis, in most cases, is thus completely preventable and curable. Yet, although the United States and most developed countries have declining rates of infection, tuberculosis has been on the rise worldwide since the 1980s, largely because many poor countries cannot afford to treat infected patients. In

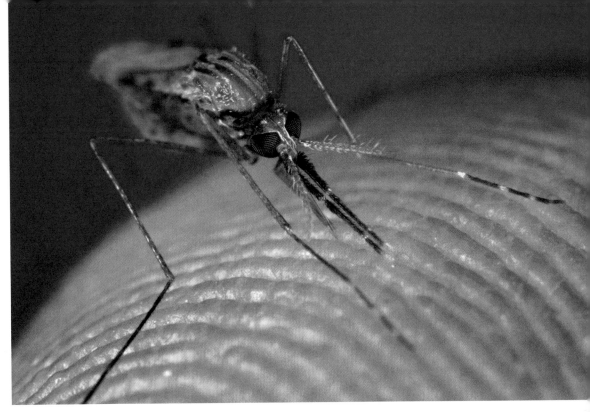

Malaria is carried from person to person by infected mosquitoes. Insecticides help control the bugs as well as the disease.

1993, the World Health Organization (WHO) declared a global tuberculosis emergency, but since then the crisis has only gotten worse. Today more than 2 million people die from tuberculosis each year.

A similar story has unfolded for malaria. French army doctor Charles Louis Alphonse Laveran first discovered that mosquitoes cause malaria in 1907. By the 1940s and 1950s, the development of the insecticide DDT and the discovery of several antimalarial drugs virtually eliminated the disease in the United States and a number of European countries. Buoyed by this success, WHO in 1957 started a program for destroying malaria worldwide, using DDT spraying and antimalarial drugs combined with monitoring efforts. By the 1960s, however, various challenges—including funding, wars, mosquitoes' resistance to insecticides, and growing drug resistance—made elimination of the disease seem impossible. In 1969, WHO abandoned its eradication program and adopted a new program that sought instead to control the disease. In the 1970s, DDT was banned for use against malaria in many countries because of its toxicity in high concentrations—a development that further hindered the global fight against malaria. Since then, the number of cases of malaria has steadily risen, and today the disease is a leading cause of death in Africa, Asia, and South America. Although it remains rare in developed nations, pockets of malaria have also broken out in Europe.

Cholera—Another Ancient Scourge Continues

Another dangerous and growing disease threat is microscopic pathogens, or infectious agents, that contaminate foods and water. Today, more than two hundred diseases are transmitted this way, causing frequent outbreaks of illness in both developed and less developed countries. Because most cases are not reported, the full scope of the problem is not known. In the United States, experts estimate that pathogens in food cause some 76 million illnesses, 325,000 hospitalizations, and at least five thousand deaths each year. Worldwide, the numbers are much larger. Global health organizations believe that hundreds of thousands of people suffer from such diseases and tens of thousands die.

Many of the deaths from food-related diseases are caused by one of the most deadly scourges from the past—cholera—which is still a health threat in many parts of the world. In the mid-1800s, a British physician, John Snow, discovered that cholera was spread by polluted water and is easily prevented by proper sanitation and hygiene. Later the cholera bacterium, *Vibrio cholerae*, was identified. Today, the disease is rare in developed countries that have modern water treatment facilities but still widespread in countries with primitive water and sewage systems and inadequate sanitation regulations. Indeed, the last cholera pandemic, which began in Indonesia in 1961, has never really ended. Instead, the disease spread to Asia, Europe, Africa, and, in 1991, to South America, where in one year it struck four hundred thousand people and caused over four thousand deaths in sixteen different countries.

Since then, the cholera pandemic has persisted. The numbers of people affected are often underreported by countries concerned about effects on tourism and trade, but each year,

Fighting Cholera the Low-Tech Way

In the 1970s, researchers discovered that cholera bacteria live in the intestines of zooplankton, microscopic life-forms that live in the ocean. This breakthrough led to an effective, low-technology way of combating cholera—filtering untreated water through ordinary cloth. This process traps much of the plankton along with the cholera bacteria, reducing the chances that people will get sick from drinking or using the water. The zooplankton discovery also led scientists to theorize that seasonal rises in ocean temperatures might produce more plankton. By monitoring plankton with satellites, Dr. Rita Colwell, an American marine microbiologist and leading expert on cholera, has confirmed that seasonal peaks in sea-surface temperatures, obtained from satellite data, correspond almost exactly with spikes in admissions for cholera in nearby hospitals. Together, these findings are helping to predict cholera outbreaks, stem the wave of cholera in developing countries, and reduce the prospects of increased cholera that could result from rising sea temperatures associated with global warming.

110,000 to 120,000 cases of cholera and about five thousand deaths are officially reported to WHO. Experts in the field claim that the real numbers today may be much higher. Making matters worse, the cholera bacteria in many places are developing a resistance to drugs such as trimethoprim, sulfamethoxazole, and streptomycin, which have historically been used to treat the infection.

Emerging Food-Borne Diseases

In the United States, the food-related illnesses that have gotten the most media attention are caused by other bacterial agents, such as *Salmonella*, *E. coli*, and *Listeria monocytogenes*. It has long been known that *Salmonella*, a type of bacteria that grows in the intestines of animals and poultry, can easily infect raw meats or eggs. If such foods are not cooked to a temperature of at least 150°F (66°C), the food can cause serious illness in humans. In 1997, for example, *Salmonella*-tainted hams served at a church fund-raising dinner in Maryland made seven hundred people ill and killed one elderly woman.

Other new food diseases have also evolved to become threats. *Escherichia coli* (or *E. coli*), for example, is a common and usually harmless type of bacteria that lives in human intestines. In 1982, however, a new, more dangerous strain of *E. coli* (called O157:H7) was identified that can cause severe stomach cramps, nausea, diarrhea, kidney damage, and sometimes death. In 1993, the O157:H7 strain created an epidemic in the Seattle, Washington, area that sickened five hundred people, mostly children, and killed at least four people. All those who fell ill had eaten undercooked, contaminated hamburgers at Jack-in-the-Box fast-food restaurants. In 1996, *E. coli* O157:H7 caused another outbreak of illness among children who drank unpasteurized apple juice produced by Odwalla Inc., a California company.

Another even more deadly food-borne pathogen, *Listeria monocytogenes*, accounts for more than five hundred deaths annually in the United States. It typically is found in meats and dairy products and can grow even in temperatures below freezing, making it the most lethal agent in the food supply. Most healthy adults will survive but the bacteria can cause death in pregnant women, unborn fetuses, and newborns. An outbreak of *Listeria monocytogenes* in eight northeastern U.S. states in 2002 infected forty-six people and caused seven deaths and three miscarriages. The victims became infected by eating contaminated turkey.

"Mad Cow Disease"

By far the scariest new food-related disease is called bovine spongiform encephalopathy. It is nicknamed "mad cow disease" because it is an infection of the brain of cows that causes bizarre symptoms such as muscle spasms, lack of muscle control, behavior problems, and eventually death. This disease for centuries was found in European sheep, but in the 1990s it jumped to cattle and then to humans, killing at least twenty people known to have eaten contaminated beef. It appears to be produced by an entirely new type of infectious agent—a form of protein called a prion that, over time, destroys healthy nerve and brain cells, leaving the brain full of holes. The outbreak decimated the European beef market and caused a ripple of fear among beef-eaters around the world. Worse yet, the infection may be lying dormant in an unknown number of people who have yet to develop symptoms of the disease. As of 2006, however, only 153 people have died from mad cow disease, most of them in Britain. Although a few cows were found to be infected with the disease on U.S. cattle ranches, no American deaths have yet been caused by the illness.

Mad cow disease is a dangerous foodborne illness. This man's son (forefront) was severely disabled after eating contaminated beef.

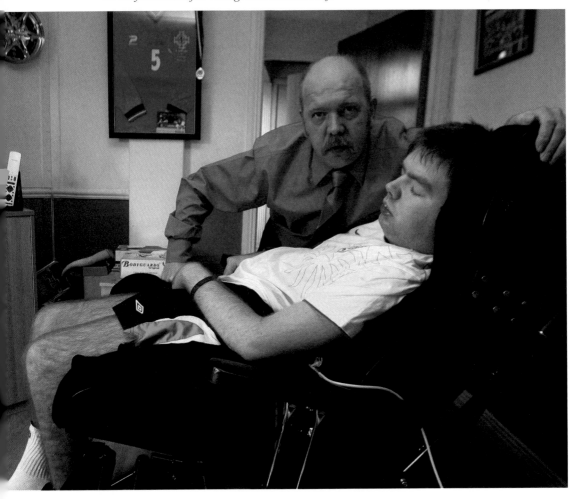

Superbugs

The growing resistance of some bacteria, often called superbugs, to antibiotics is a growing concern in both developed and undeveloped countries, including the United States. Researchers' biggest worry today is defending against several very commonplace forms of bacteria—*Streptococci, Staphylococcus aureus*, and *Enterococci*—all of which can cause life-threatening illnesses if they are not treated.

THE TOP KILLER

"Infectious diseases remain the number one killer of humans worldwide."

Michael T. Osterholm, infectious disease expert. Michael T. Osterholm, "Preparing for the Next Pandemic," *Foreign Affairs*, July–August 2005, p. 4.

Streptococci bacteria, for example, are responsible for a host of diseases, including strep throat, scarlet fever, rheumatic fever, and bacterial pneumonia. On rare occasions, they can invade the whole body, triggering a disease called necrotizing fasciitis, often called flesh-eating strep because it rapidly rots the flesh away, sometimes causing the loss of an arm or leg within hours. Another type of bacteria, *Staphylococcus aureus*, produces serious skin and soft tissue infections (called staph infections); if it enters the bloodstream, it can cause heart valve, blood, and bone infections and can lead to septic shock and death. *Enterococci* bacteria are the leading cause of surgical wound infections and can cause a range of other problems, including urinary tract infections and infections of the bloodstream, heart valves, and brain. All these bacteria are commonly found in hospitals, where they often attack very ill patients whose immune systems are already weakened.

Since the discovery of antibiotics, these bacteria have been easily controlled by antibiotic medicines. Over recent decades, however, all three microbes have become increasingly resistant to most antibiotics. Today, only one antibiotic, vancomycin, remains consistently effective against these infections, and the concern is that one day even this drug of last resort will no longer work. Already, rare strains of staph and *Enteroccoci* bacteria have emerged that show resistance to vancomycin. Such resistance, if it becomes widespread, would wreak havoc in health care facilities and endanger the lives of millions of hospital patients. Medical journalist Madeline Drexler warns:

> A shadow would fall across medicine. Surgeons would think twice before doing elective procedures, from hip replacements to cyst removal, for fear of life-threatening complications. More people would die in hospitals: intensive care patients, surgical wound patients, dialysis patients, transplant patients, even otherwise healthy patients who happen to get a staph infection from an IV. . . . At least a quarter of the 50,000 serious hospital staph infections each year [in the United States] would be fatal. Health care workers could become potential carriers and a threat to patients. . . . With hospitals whipping up armies of totally and near totally resistant bacteria, what worries public health officials is that these armies may venture outside [to homes, schools, and workplaces].[13]

Medical experts fervently hope this day does not come, but infectious disease clearly continues to be one of mankind's most difficult challenges.

FIGHTING TODAY'S PANDEMICS

Several of the diseases that emerged in the late twentieth century are now spreading around the globe. In the new millennium, AIDS/HIV has become a true pandemic, raging throughout most of the world. Tuberculosis and malaria, too, have reached pandemic levels, and several new diseases have also raised fears of worldwide contagion. Most affected are undeveloped countries in Africa and Asia, which lack the resources to combat these lethal infectious diseases. The world's record in fighting these threats has been, at best, mixed.

Fighting the AIDS/HIV Pandemic

The status of the AIDS/HIV pandemic is grim. In the twenty-five years since AIDS/HIV was first identified, more than eight hundred thousand cases of infection have been reported in the United States, and about half a million Americans have died. Many more are infected but are hiding it or do not know they have the disease. By 1996 AIDS had become the leading cause of death among American men age twenty-five to forty-five, and for women in this age group, it is the third leading cause of death. AIDS has spread even more rapidly in less developed areas of the world. According to estimates from global health organizations, 42 million people in the world now have AIDS and more than 20 million have died from the disease. Every day, some eighty-five hundred people die of AIDS; each year, the death toll is about 3 million.

Africa is one of the worst-hit regions. There, about 24.5 million people are AIDS-infected, or one in every forty people. Indeed, the disease in African nations has become the leading cause of death for both men and women, and it is wiping out much of an entire generation of parents and laborers, leaving behind many orphaned children. Karen Stanecki, chief of health studies for the U.S. Census Bureau, explains, "People are dying in the years when they're supposed to be most productive, and they won't be there to raise the next generation. Which means you'll have all these orphans and no one to raise them."[14] AIDS

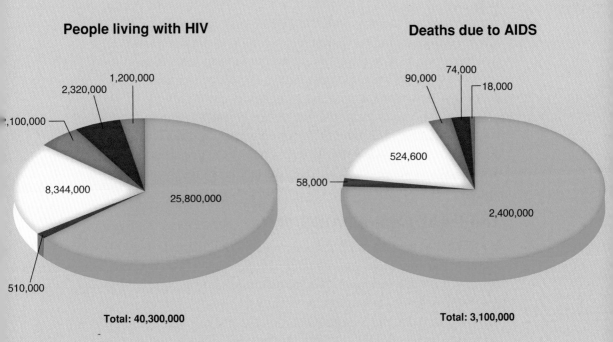

HIV/AIDS Status Worldwide

People living with HIV

1,200,000
2,320,000
,100,000
8,344,000
25,800,000
510,000

Total: 40,300,000

Deaths due to AIDS

74,000
90,000
18,000
524,600
58,000
2,400,000

Total: 3,100,000

As of November 2005, an estimated 40.3 million adults and children around the world were living with the HIV virus, and about 3.1 million people died of AIDS in 2005.

One particular region of the world has been very hard hit. Two-thirds of all people living with HIV and 90 percent of all AIDS orphans are from sub-Saharan Africa.

Sub-Saharan Africa
North Africa and Middle East
Asia and Oceania
Latin America and Caribbean
Europe and Central Asia
North America

Source: UNAIDS (The Joint United Nations Programme on HIV/AIDS; www.unaids.org).

is also believed to be ravaging Asia, although exact numbers are unavailable. The disease is just beginning to hit Russia and is soon expected to explode in India and China, the world's two most populous nations. Health experts believe that by 2010, as many as 100 million people around the world will have AIDS.

In addition to this heavy human toll, AIDS will likely produce significant social, economic, and political changes that could have grave consequences for the United States and the rest of the world. Developing countries whose populations and economies are decimated by the virus can be expected to become even poorer and more socially and politically unstable, creating conditions that may lead to future wars or terrorist activities. In Russia, the pressures of dealing with the disease may further threaten an already tenuous plan for democracy. China and India, meanwhile, may see their now remarkable economic growth fade as they absorb the costs of an AIDS pandemic. Indeed, the entire world economy may be weakened as countries lose their ability to import and export essential products. The destabilizing effects of AIDS may also threaten the ability of countries with nuclear arms, such as India, to control the spread of nuclear materials and technology. AIDS expert Greg Behrman warns that AIDS is "the defining humanitarian catastrophe of our time."[15]

The Fight Against AIDS/HIV

Yet the battle against AIDS has been marked by denial, discrimination, and moral judgments, and in some ways it has only just begun. In the United States, the government at first met the disease with silence and inaction. Although the disease was first reported in 1981, U.S. president Ronald Reagan did not even mention the word *AIDS* in public until 1986. Monies were not allocated to fight the disease; instead, the government took largely negative actions such as banning immigrants who were HIV-positive. Socially, the 1980s were a time when people with AIDS faced enormous prejudices. Even though the disease cannot be spread through everyday contact, many infected people lost their jobs and were shunned by friends and loved ones.

In the 1990s, however, government agencies in the United States began funding research, approving drug therapies, and

Ryan White—the AIDS Poster Boy

Ryan White was a middle-class teenager from the United States who became a hero around the world because of his brave battle against AIDS. Ryan contracted AIDS at age thirteen from infusions of infected blood, which he needed to treat hemophilia, a medical condition in which the blood fails to clot properly. At that time, AIDS was viewed as a disease of homosexual men, and Ryan encountered much discrimination and prejudice because of his AIDS diagnosis. Even though AIDS cannot be spread from casual contact, he was expelled from his school because of fear that he could spread the disease to other students. Ryan sued the school and won, but his family decided to move to a new town, where he was warmly welcomed. During the rest of his life, Ryan worked to educate people about AIDS. He was a guest on television talk shows and became internationally known. He died on April 8, 1990, and his funeral was attended by fifteen hundred people, including celebrities such as singer Michael Jackson. A few months later, a new federal law, called the Ryan White CARE Act, was enacted to improve health care for people with HIV/AIDS.

Young Ryan White was much admired for his battle against AIDS.

providing information about the illness. As a result, new drugs such as AZT began to prolong the lives of people living with AIDS, and antidiscrimination legislation and awareness campaigns began to lessen the stigma of AIDS and prevent new infections. AIDS-related deaths declined substantially in America by the late 1990s. The same gains were seen in other industrialized areas, such as Europe.

DEATH BY AIDS

"By 2020, the AIDS virus will have caused more deaths than any disease outbreak in history—including the Black Death in fourteenth-century Europe, which mowed down one-third of the population."

Madeline Drexler, science and medical journalist. Madeline Drexler, *Secret Agents: The Menace of Emerging Infections.* Washington, DC: Joseph Henry, 2002, p. 282.

The world's poorest and least developed countries, however, have been largely left to fend for themselves. These developing nations have not implemented AIDS prevention and health education programs, and less than 1 percent of infected people receive anti-AIDS drug therapies. Law professor and public health scholar Lawrence O. Gostin explains, "More than ever, the AIDS pandemic has created two worlds—one with relatively low burdens of disease and sophisticated treatments and the other with staggering burdens and paltry health care resources."[16]

Although the United States has been the largest contributor to global efforts to fight AIDS and the biggest source of help for Africa, its efforts have been criticized as inadequate and weakened by moral constraints. USAID, America's main international aid agency, has donated almost $6 billion in HIV/AIDS funding to almost one hundred countries around the world since 1986, more than any other public or private organization. Critics charge, however, that the administration of U.S. president George W. Bush has been unduly influenced by Christian fundamentalists to give more grants to religious groups, who favor religious policies such as abstinence from sex until marriage, than to secular groups who promote proven prevention methods. In addition, $6 billion is only a tiny fraction of the hundreds of billions that the United States spends for other priorities, such as the war and reconstruction in Iraq, and a small part of what is needed internationally for AIDS. The United Nations' AIDS program, called UNAIDS, estimates that at least $15 billion is needed each year to fight AIDS in poor and middle-income countries. This figure is expected to rise in the future as AIDS penetrates more and more countries around the globe.

In 2003, Bush promised $15 billion in AIDS funding over five years, and as of early 2006, Congress had authorized about $5 billion of this amount. Many people hope that this increased commitment, combined with help from other countries, will begin to stem the tide of the AIDS pandemic. Others remain skeptical about the future, noting that the annual amount donated now worldwide will have to increase very quickly and dramatically to have any real effect on the spread of AIDS. Lawrence Gostin explains, "What is still needed are the economic resources and political will necessary to implement comprehensive programs for AIDS prevention and treatment in every region."[17]

Dealing with TB and Malaria

AIDS/HIV is not the only disease that today fits the definition of a pandemic. Tuberculosis now infects nearly one-third of the world's population, or about 2 billion people. Altogether, nearly 3 million die from the disease every year. Even in the United States, more than twenty thousand TB cases arise annually, mostly because of the large numbers of people traveling from other countries. Many of those infected will never get sick because their immune systems are able to fight the TB infection, but tuberculosis is often a death sentence for people whose immune systems have been weakened by other diseases such as the AIDS/HIV virus. In Africa and India, where there is a high incidence of AIDS/HIV, TB has become the leading cause of death among HIV-positive people, creating a growing humanitarian crisis. Indeed, experts say that the combination of AIDS and TB has created one of the greatest health threats in human history.

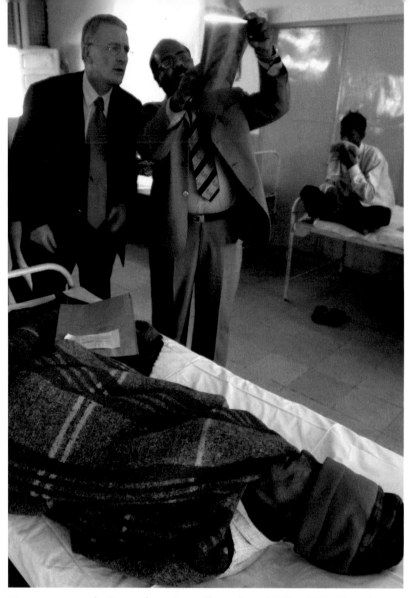

Doctors examine the X-ray of a patient suffering from AIDS and TB. TB is a huge threat to HIV-positive people in India and Africa.

The great tragedy of the TB pandemic is that the disease is usually preventable with vaccines and curable in almost 95 percent of cases if patients are given the correct dose of inexpensive antituberculosis drugs. Such health care is readily available in wealthy, industrialized countries, but in much of the developing world, health care systems are poor or nonexistent, and many TB victims die simply because neither they nor their governments can afford lifesaving drugs. Even worse, in some areas such as Russia, there is a growing incidence of drug-resistant varieties of TB, making treatment difficult even if drugs are available. As researchers Mathew Gandy and Alimuddin Zumla put it, "The history of TB is a story of medical failure."[18]

After AIDS and TB, malaria is the world's third leading killer. The disease now kills more than three thousand people each day and more than a million annually. The poor and vulnerable, especially pregnant women and children, are the most at risk. In Africa, where AIDS and TB are rampant among the adult population, malaria kills one child in twenty before the age of five. The disease

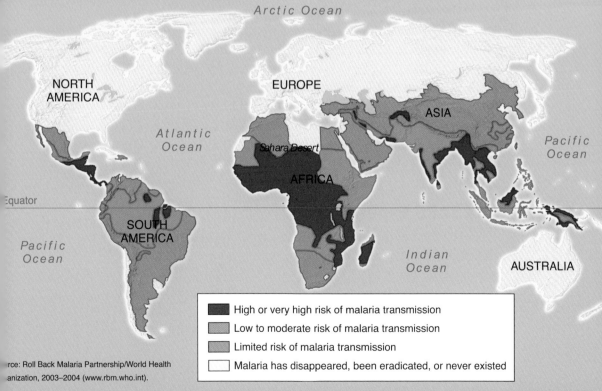

Malaria Transmission Risk

Malaria is transmitted across the tropical and subtropical regions of our planet (these are regions with hot climates, close to the equator). These regions also happen to include some of the world's poorest countries.

Approximately 40 percent of the world's population is at risk for contracting malaria. Ninety percent of malaria deaths occur in Africa south of the Sahara desert; most of those who die are young children.

- High or very high risk of malaria transmission
- Low to moderate risk of malaria transmission
- Limited risk of malaria transmission
- Malaria has disappeared, been eradicated, or never existed

Source: Roll Back Malaria Partnership/World Health Organization, 2003–2004 (www.rbm.who.int).

often causes death in less than twenty-four hours. Like TB, however, malaria can be easily and inexpensively controlled. Simple precautions such as spraying insecticides or installing mosquito netting help to prevent infection, and a cocktail of antimalarial drugs can usually cure, or at least subdue, the disease. Many antimalarial drugs, however, are losing their effectiveness due to improper use. Today, a drug called artemisinin has become the leading treatment, but it should be used in combination with older medications. Many countries, however, are buying only artemisinin, and scientists worry that use of artemisinin alone will cause even this drug to lose its potency. This drug resistance comes at the same time that insect carriers of malaria are becoming resistant to common insecticides. These challenges make malaria as formidable an enemy as TB and highlight the need for a malaria vaccine that could prevent all infection.

As is the case with AIDS/HIV, the main obstacle in fighting TB and malaria is funding that can come only from developed nations. The United States, through USAID, has contributed millions to fight TB and malaria since 1998, but more money is clearly needed. An international organization, called the Global Fund for AIDS, TB, and Malaria, was created in 2001 to finance the fight against these three major diseases, but critics say that contributions to the organization have so far been anemic. For fiscal year 2006, the Bush administration proposed giving $300 million to the fund, but many critics say twice as much is needed. Health experts agree that only a massive, well-funded attack will turn the tide of these diseases. An October 2005 editorial in the *Boston Globe* newspaper emphasizes, "To achieve its goals, [the Global Fund] needs adequate support from wealthy nations."[19]

The SARS Experience

Since the turn of the twenty-first century, the world has also faced the prospect of a pandemic from a completely new disease— severe acute respiratory syndrome (SARS). Caused by a type of virus called a coronavirus, SARS is a highly virulent and contagious form of pneumonia that produces flu-like symptoms of cough, sore throat, muscle aches, lethargy, and high fever. SARS kills about 10 percent of its victims. An epidemic of the disease first arose in November 2002 in China. The virus may have jumped from wildlife to humans; the prime animal suspect was the civet cat, a wild, weasel-like mammal widely sold in Chinese food markets.

China, however, failed to reveal the outbreak to the rest of the world until February 2003, when news leaked out about an American business traveler who came down with symptoms on a flight to Singapore. The plane was forced to stop in Vietnam, where the man was hospitalized and later died, but only after infecting several of the doctors and nurses treating him. The incident alarmed international health officials and led to the issuance of a global SARS alert on March 12, 2003. Partly because

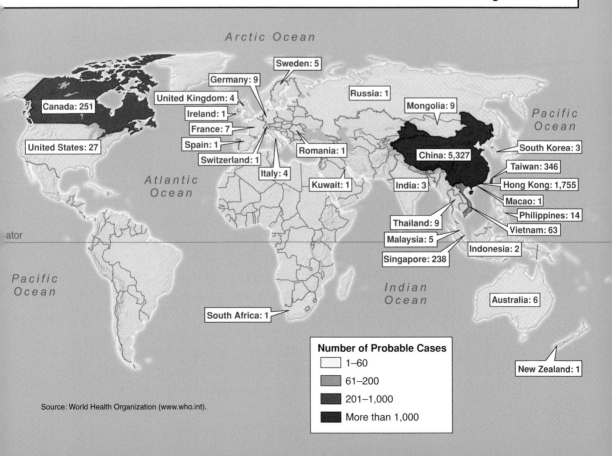

Number of Probable SARS Cases, November 2002–July 2003

Arctic Ocean

Sweden: 5
Germany: 9
United Kingdom: 4
Ireland: 1
Canada: 251
France: 7
Spain: 1
Switzerland: 1
Russia: 1
Mongolia: 9
United States: 27
Romania: 1
China: 5,327
South Korea: 3
Italy: 4
Kuwait: 1
India: 3
Taiwan: 346
Hong Kong: 1,755
Macao: 1
Philippines: 14
Thailand: 9
Vietnam: 63
Malaysia: 5
Indonesia: 2
Singapore: 238
Pacific Ocean
Atlantic Ocean
Pacific Ocean
Indian Ocean
Australia: 6
South Africa: 1
New Zealand: 1

Number of Probable Cases
- 1–60
- 61–200
- 201–1,000
- More than 1,000

Source: World Health Organization (www.who.int).

of China's failure to immediately warn other countries about SARS, the disease spread rapidly to other parts of Asia, such as Hong Kong and Vietnam, and even as far away as Canada. In fact, thanks to modern international travel, SARS spread to five countries within twenty-four hours and to thirty countries on six continents within several months. The rapid movement of the deadly disease spread fears around the world of a pandemic that might be as bad as the 1918 flu. Professor Alfred J. Bollett explains, "A public reaction close to panic developed."[20]

Once SARS was revealed, however, the world health community responded swiftly by investigating, identifying the cause of the disease, and implementing public health measures that were soon successful in stopping it. Strict quarantines were imposed in Hong Kong, Singapore, Taiwan, and Canada to restrict infected people to their homes. In some of these areas, schools and businesses were closed, and selected hospitals were designated as SARS facilities to keep SARS-infected patients from infecting large numbers of people. Many countries around the world also began screening airline passengers to eliminate travelers who were suspected of having the disease. In China, officials destroyed over ten thousand civet cats, which were believed to be carriers of the SARS virus. By July 2003, health officials declared that the SARS danger was over, but new cases of the disease were recorded later in 2003 and in 2004. No cases were reported in 2005.

Altogether, SARS infected over eight thousand people and caused more than eight hundred deaths. SARS also devastated the Asian economy, resulting in losses of about $40 billion, as tourism declined dramatically and people canceled travel plans and business conventions due to their fear of SARS. Despite these losses, however, many experts believe that the aggressive response to SARS stemmed what could have evolved into a much larger pandemic.

Dangers from Hemorrhagic Fevers

Another worrisome development in recent years has been the emergence of a number of new mystery viruses that cause various forms of hemorrhagic fevers—diseases with frightening symptoms that can produce death within six to nine days. These diseases strike the body's vascular, or blood circulation, system and are often accompanied by massive hemorrhaging, or bleeding, that practically liquefies internal organs. Michael B.A. Oldstone, a professor of immunology at the Scripps Research Institute, explains, "Once infected with any of these viruses, the victim soon suffers profuse breaks in small blood vessels, causing blood to ooze from the skin, mouth, and rectum. Internally, blood flows into the pleural cavity where the lungs are located, into the pericardial cavity surrounding the heart, into the abdomen, and into organs like the liver, kidney, heart, spleen, and lungs. Eventually this uncontrolled bleeding causes . . . death."[21] Experts suspect that hemorrhagic fevers are transmitted through contact with infected animals or insects. Infected victims become highly contagious, easily spreading the diseases to others.

Hemorrhagic fever viruses produce a variety of different forms of disease that go by different names. One hemorrhagic virus found in the United States, for example, is hantavirus—an infectious agent common in the wild deer mouse, a small creature that lives in most parts of the country. Although this virus has probably existed in deer mice for centuries, U.S. health officials in recent years have begun to record episodes of hantaviruses crossing over to humans. One of the first such cases occurred in 1993 on the Navajo Indian reservation in Muerto Canyon, New Mexico. Two healthy adults—a man and a woman —suddenly became acutely ill with high fever, muscle pain, and cough, and they both died a few days later after their lungs filled with fluid. A number of similar cases were soon uncovered in New Mexico and three neighboring states. By mid-1995, 106 cases of this hantavirus were recorded in some twenty American states, and over half of those infected had died.

Eventually, researchers concluded that people get the disease when they inhale tiny infected particles of deer mouse urine or droppings. There is no cure or vaccine, and the only method of prevention is controlling the numbers of deer mice near populated areas. This task of prevention becomes more difficult following periods of heavy rains and mild temperatures—conditions that produce more food for the mice and trigger deer mice population explosions. Even during periods of hantavirus outbreaks, however, the total number of people affected has been small, making this disease one of the least likely to produce a widespread pandemic.

THE EBOLA THREAT

"The fear and fascination attached to Ebola outbreaks comes from our ignorance of how to treat, prevent, or contain the disease, and our helplessness in its wake."

Michael B.A. Oldstone, immunologist. Michael B.A. Oldstone, *Viruses, Plagues, and History*. New York: Oxford University Press, 1998, p. 135.

Two much more dangerous hemorrhagic fevers are Ebola and Lassa fever, both of which emerged in Africa. The first Ebola outbreak occurred in Zaire (later renamed the Democratic Republic of the Congo) in 1976, where it infected 318 persons and killed

Other Emerging Infections

In recent decades, a number of new bacterial diseases emerged in the United States. Lyme disease first appeared in Old Lyme, Connecticut, in 1975. It is caused by Borrelia burgdorferi bacteria and is transmitted to humans by the bite of infected ticks. Lyme disease has been reported in all regions of the United States, but it is most common in northeastern states. The infection can cause chronic joint pain, arthritis, fatigue, and neurological problems. Legionnaires' disease, also known as Legionellosis, is a rare form of pneumonia that first appeared in 1976 at a convention of the American Legion, an organization for ex-servicemen, in Philadelphia, Pennsylvania. During that first outbreak, 221 people contracted the disease and thirty-four died. The disease is caused by inhaling bacteria that often grow in air conditioning systems. Another serious bacterial infection, toxic shock syndrome, is caused by Staphylococcus aureus (or staph) bacteria. It first appeared in 1980, when it was associated with the use of tampons by menstruating women. However, the disease can also occur in anyone who has any type of staph infection, such as pneumonia or a wound infection. All three diseases are treated with antibiotics.

280, or 88 percent. Years later, in 1995, Ebola erupted again in Zaire (in a populous city called Kikwit), where it infected at least 316 people, this time killing 244, or 77 percent. Officials suspect that these numbers are low, however, because many infected people undoubtedly died in surrounding rural villages without reporting their illness. Most of those who died were young adults.

The outbreak in Kikwit caused great panic, and the army imposed a quarantine by sealing off roads, preventing residents from leaving the city. Hospitals filled with patients, but no treatment was available, and the disease quickly killed not only the patients, but also their families and the doctors and nurses treating them. Zaire's government sent an urgent plea for help to international health experts, who investigated the cause of the illness and imposed quarantines on anyone known to have been in Kikwit during the outbreak. Scientists, however, still know very little about Ebola and there are no cures or vaccines. Outbreaks continue to occur in different parts of Africa even today.

Lassa fever is a similarly lethal disease that first arose in 1969 in West Africa and has had numerous outbreaks since then. Like Ebola, it often causes death, at rates as high as 60 percent of those infected. Also like Ebola, not much is known about Lassa fever, due to the lack of research or monitoring in the areas of Africa where it is occurring. The main concern of health experts who study Ebola, Lassa, and other remote hemorrhagic fevers is that they could mutate and easily spread to more populated parts of the world, such as the Americas, Europe, and Asia. So far, these exotic viruses have not made the leap to other regions, but they continue to present a risk of possible pandemic proportions.

Lessons Learned

The experience of trying to respond to old and new diseases that can spread quickly around the world has produced some lessons in the new reality of infectious disease. AIDS/HIV has shown, for example, that delaying disease prevention and control efforts because of cultural or social shame risks lives and prevents effective action that could stop the spread of infectious disease. Another important message is that only concerted efforts and good health care can prevent the spread of diseases such as AIDS/HIV, TB, and malaria. For developing countries and their poverty-stricken populations, this requires a large infusion of foreign aid from wealthy, industrialized countries.

The biggest lesson from the SARS epidemics, meanwhile, is the need for countries experiencing onslaughts of new diseases to report such illnesses immediately to international health authorities to lessen the chance of a potential pandemic. Health experts hope that China, for example, has learned from SARS that concerns about tourism, trade, and national honor are not nearly as important as protecting the health of the planet's human population. In today's world of international travel and global trade, only quick responses by international public health officials can hope to isolate newly emerging, highly contagious diseases.

The danger of acquiring disease from wild and domestic animals has also been driven home by the recent outbreaks of

Indian women march at an AIDS/HIV awareness rally. Cultural shame can slow a community's progress in fighting the disease.

SARS and hemorrhagic fevers. Experts say that in coming years populations of wild animals near human settlements, as well as domestic cows, chickens, and sheep, should be monitored for disease in order to prevent infected animals from entering the food chain or coming into close contact with humans. Human settlement and other activities can create new opportunities for infectious microorganisms to attack and spread among humans, and in response, humankind must act aggressively to prevent and control disease outbreaks.

FUTURE PANDEMIC
THREATS

Health experts are now concerned about several possible diseases and biological threats that could produce the next pandemic. These include not only new varieties of disease, such as the much-talked-about avian flu, but also the increasing risk of known infectious agents being accidentally introduced into human population centers and, even worse, the intentional use of deadly microbes as a biological weapon of war or terror. Any of these scenarios could have catastrophic results in today's interconnected world.

Anthrax Bioterrorism

In recent years, especially after the terrorist strike on the United States on September 11, 2001, many people have awakened to the dangers of biological terror—attacks on civilians caused by the intentional release of deadly diseases in densely populated areas. Experts have warned that if terrorists are willing to use them, viruses and bacteria can be highly effective instruments of mass destruction. Journalist Madeline Drexler explains,

> Unlike nuclear or chemical weapons, [biological weapons] self-propagate and adapt. They jump continents with ease. And a small amount can cause vast damage. . . . [Also] in a bioterrorist assault, health officials . . . may not notice until too late. Because pathogens require an incubation period to multiply in the body before they trigger symptoms, the first sign could occur days or weeks after the attack. By that time, the trail would be cold, and it might be impossible to determine if the epidemic was a freak event or a malicious act of aggression.[22]

One of the most deadly bioterrorism agents is anthrax, a common and highly lethal type of bacteria that kills 80 percent of its victims. Anthrax spreads through hardy spores that can be easily released into the air. If inhaled by humans, anthrax first causes mild fever and fatigue and then quickly releases toxins into the bloodstream that destroy tissues and blood vessels. Fluid accumulates in tissues, blood vessels leak blood, and patients soon cannot breathe, leading in most cases to rapid death. Antibiotics can be used against anthrax, but they are most effective before symptoms appear. Vaccines also have been developed, but the United States maintains only a small supply of the anthrax vaccine and reserves it for military use.

Anthrax spores are so tough that they can survive for decades, making anthrax a perfect candidate for germ warfare.

Hazardous-materials workers clean up outside the U.S. Senate building after a bioterrorist anthrax infection in 2001.

In fact, many countries, such as the Soviet Union, have manufactured and stockpiled anthrax as part of biowarfare programs, and the bacteria also live naturally in soils around the world. The abundance of sources means that anthrax is widely available to terrorists.

Other Bioterrorist Threats

The United States got a small taste of the dangers of anthrax bioterrorism in September and October 2001, when five letters containing anthrax were mailed to news media offices and two U.S. senators. Twenty-two people developed anthrax infections and five died—one a photo editor for a Florida newspaper, two postal employees, and two people whose mail was likely contaminated by contact with the anthrax letters. As of 2006, the government has been unable to determine who was behind the deadly attacks, but there is some evidence that the anthrax may have come from U.S. military laboratories.

An even more dangerous pathogen that could be used by terrorists is the smallpox virus, which has killed millions of people since ancient times. Although smallpox disease was eradicated in all parts of the world by 1980, small stockpiles of the virus are maintained in two official and carefully guarded laboratories, one in the United States and one in Russia, for research purposes. Experts, however, believe that other laboratories both inside and outside Russia secretly hold samples of smallpox virus, and their security status is unknown. Many health authorities have urged that all stocks of smallpox be destroyed, but this has not occurred. In 2001, for example, U.S. president George Bush decided to retain U.S. samples for further research.

If terrorists somehow manage to acquire some of the smallpox virus and release it as part of a terrorist attack, the result could be calamitous. Smallpox is highly contagious and could infect populations around the world with breathtaking speed. As many as half of those infected could die, but only after suffering through horrible symptoms such as seeping lesions and bleeding. The sick would infect many others, including health care workers, and total panic would likely ensue. Michael Osterholm, director of the Center for Infectious Disease Research and Policy, has stated, "If there was even a very limited release of smallpox in a public setting today . . . it would be the closest thing to a living hell we've probably ever known."[23]

There is a vaccine for smallpox, but today, even those who were vaccinated in the past have lost their immunity to the disease. Following the anthrax scare in 2001, the U.S. government authorized the manufacture and stockpiling of enough smallpox vaccine to vaccinate every American if it becomes necessary. Many poorer countries, however, have no smallpox vaccine program and would probably be decimated in a smallpox pandemic.

Numerous other biological agents could also be used as weapons, including hemorrhagic fever viruses, ricin (a toxin derived from common castor beans), and even the ancient plague bacteria, which is still widely available to researchers. With newly developing gene technology, researchers recreated the 1918 flu virus, publishing their analysis in October 2005. Some scientists praised this work, arguing that it will help them to spot the next pandemic flu and develop new flu vaccines, but other researchers say that the public dissemination of the genetic makeup of such a deadly virus raises the risk it could be used for purposes of terror. Richard Ebright, a bacteriologist at Rutgers University, warns, "[Researchers] have constructed, and provided procedures for others to construct, a virus that represents perhaps the most effective bioweapons agent now known."[24]

In the future, scientists could even create new, more lethal pathogens by splicing together genes from different deadly organisms. One of the most frightening possibilities is the creation of a new virus that could cripple the body's immune system or the development of new forms of common viruses or bacteria that would resist current antibiotic drugs and vaccines. Terrorists could also attack agriculture or domestic animal farms, poisoning a nation's or even the world's food supply.

An Increasing Bioterrorist Threat

Many experts say that the prospects of a bioterror attack are increasing. Today, as many as seventeen nations, including Iran, North Korea, China, and Syria, are suspected of having biological

Bioterror Attack in Japan

One of the few bioterrorist attacks recorded to date occurred in 1995 in Tokyo, Japan. During the morning rush hour, five members of a religious sect called Aum Shinrikyo deposited packages of the deadly nerve gas sarin on board commuter trains, then quietly walked away. As the trains continued on their way, gas slowly began leaking out, and people trapped on the moving trains could not escape the terrifying poison. The gas made more than five thousand people sick, almost five hundred were admitted to hospitals with serious injuries, and twelve people died. Five years later, two cult members involved in the incident, Yasuo Hayashi and Masato Yokoyama, were sentenced to death, and several others received sentences of life in prison. Although the effects were not catastrophic, the attack brought worldwide attention to the threat of biological terror.

Rescue workers assist injured passengers after the 1995 nerve-gas attack in Tokyo.

weapons programs. Such weapons have been described as the "poor man's atomic bombs" because they can be developed more cheaply and with less sophisticated technology than nuclear weapons. Some of the countries on the bioterror list are considered by the United States to be state sponsors of terrorism, and some have contacts with known terrorist groups. So far, the instances of assaults using biological weapons have been small both in number and scale, but given the spread of technology, experts say that more widespread use of bioterror by governments or terrorist groups is perhaps only a matter of time.

Dangers from Lab Accidents

As more and more researchers work in laboratories around the world on biological warfare and antiterror projects, health experts are also becoming increasingly concerned about the danger of an accidental release of a deadly pathogen that could spark a pandemic. Even the most careful medical researchers make mistakes, and the chances of a lab worker being infected and spreading disease, or of viruses or bacteria being inadvertently released due to some breakdown in lab security, may be quite high. Richard Ebright, for example, believes that there is a significant risk, "verging on inevitability," of deadly viruses being accidentally released into the human population or stolen by a "disgruntled, disturbed or extremist laboratory employee."[25]

In April 1979, these fears came true when an explosion at a secret military installation near the Russian city of Sverdlovsk released anthrax bacteria into the air, killing at least sixty-eight people living nearby. The Soviet Union denied the news reports of the incident for years, but Russian president Boris Yeltsin finally admitted in 1992 that the deaths were caused by an accidental release of the disease microbes from a lab that was producing anthrax as part of a Russian bioweapons military program.

Another close call came in late November 1989, when Ebola virus was found in monkeys that were brought into the United States for research purposes by Hazelton Research Products, an American company. When the monkeys began dying, the company's veterinarian suspected that they had a type of hemorrhagic fever seen only in monkeys. When researchers examined

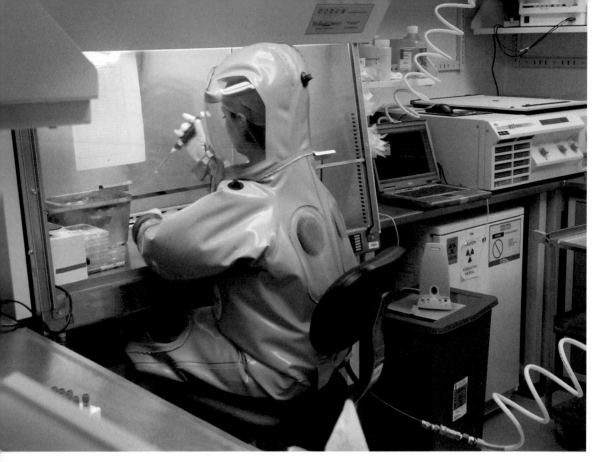

A scientist works in the U.S. Army's medical laboratory. Germs must be handled with extreme care to avoid accidental release.

the monkeys' blood, however, they found the Ebola virus, which can be deadly to humans. With this frightening finding, all the Hazelton monkeys suspected of having the disease were quickly euthanized and health authorities required everyone who might have come in contact with the monkeys or their blood or tissue specimens to be monitored for illness. Several of the Hazelton workers were found to be infected with the Ebola virus, but curiously, none of them became ill. No one understands why this strain of Ebola did not cause disease in humans, but health authorities were thankful that, in this instance at least, an epidemic spread of Ebola was averted.

Numerous other potential biological accidents have also been publicized in recent years. Although the SARS outbreak was brought under control quickly, several smaller subsequent outbreaks of SARS occurred in 2003 and 2004 due to the accidental

The 1976 Swine Flu Scare

In 1976, an outbreak of a new strain of influenza caused U.S. health officials to fear a possible pandemic. It was called the swine flu because it was a type of virus usually found in domestic and wild pigs, or swine. The outbreak began in February 1976, when a young U.S. army recruit stationed at Fort Dix, New Jersey, suddenly fell ill from the infection and died within twenty-four hours. Four more soldiers were hospitalized, and another five hundred soldiers caught swine flu but did not get sick. Doctors and public health officials worried that any infection that could spread that fast might evolve into a world-wide plague. By mid-March, the Centers for Disease Control (CDC) called on President Gerald Ford to support a $135 million program to vaccinate all 220 million Americans. Although only one person had died from the new flu, the government authorized the massive program and insulated drug companies from liability for any potentially harmful side effects. Over 40 million people were vaccinated but the program was stopped early because hundreds of people began experiencing side effects that included heart attacks and neurological problems. Some who received the vaccine died.

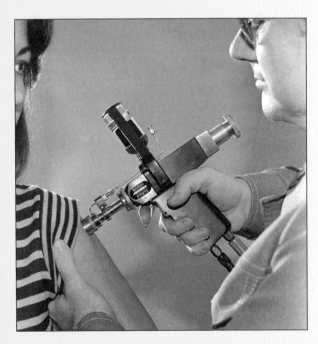

A doctor injects a patient with the swine flu vaccine.

release of the SARS virus from laboratories in Taiwan, Singapore, and China. In another case, an accidental release of the Marburg virus, a cousin of Ebola, in Angola in 2003 caused an outbreak among the local population that killed more than two hundred people.

A Random Event

"To the best of our knowledge, influenza pandemics are rare, random events. You're never 'overdue' for a random event."

Richard Schabas, former chief medical officer of Ontario, Canada. Quoted in David Stipp, "Is the Risk Overblown? Calling a Pandemic 'Overdue' Is a Misnomer Worthy of Chicken Little," *Fortune*, March 7, 2005, p. 120.

One of the most recent mistakes involving lethal infectious agents occurred in April 2005 in the United States. A U.S. biotech company, Meridian Bioscience Inc., accidentally sent samples of a deadly flu—a type called H2N2 or the Asian flu, which killed more than seventy thousand Americans in 1957–1958—to over five thousand laboratories in the United States and sixteen other countries around the world. No one has yet been infected, but because this flu virus has not existed outside labs since 1968, anyone under the age of thirty-seven would lack immunity and be completely susceptible. U.S. health authorities asked all the affected labs to immediately destroy their samples of H2N2, but compliance with the request cannot be enforced, and chances are good that samples still exist. Health reporter Debora MacKenzie points out, "The [H2N2] incident underscore[d] the risk that the next flu pandemic might come . . . from a laboratory."[26]

Avian Flu—The Most Likely Future Pandemic

According to experts, however, the most likely and most feared pandemic today is one that may be caused not by human error but by a naturally occurring virus—specifically, a new type of influenza virus that causes a disease called bird, or avian, flu. Concerns about an avian flu pandemic first arose in the 1990s, when the new flu strain named H5N1 (after two proteins, hemagglutinin and neuraminidase, that make up the exterior of the virus) began appearing in the poultry populations of Asia. At first, like other avian diseases, this flu caused very mild symptoms, such as reduced egg production, in domestic birds. Quickly, however, the disease evolved into a deadly flu that killed virtually 100 percent of all birds that it infected, usually within forty-eight hours.

Since then, cases of bird flu have been reported in various places around the world, suggesting that the disease is spreading, probably along the migration routes of wild birds. As wild birds make stopovers to rest or to look for food and water, they come into contact with domestic birds, thus spreading the bird flu infection to chickens, ducks, geese, pigeons, and turkeys. Outbreaks among domestic birds have now been recorded in South Korea, Vietnam, Japan, Thailand, Cambodia, Lao People's Democratic Republic, Indonesia, China, Mongolia, Russia, Turkey, Iraq, and Nigeria, as well as in European countries including Italy, Greece, Germany, Austria, France, and Switzerland.

CRYING WOLF

"Many people are crying wolf when it comes to the avian virus."

Peter Palese, chair of microbiology at Mount Sinai School of Medicine in New York. Quoted in Ronald Bailey, "The End of Pandemics: Bird Flu Could Be the Last Super-Plague," *ReasonOnline*, November 11, 2005. www.reason.com/rb/rb111105.shtml.

So far, the main response of health officials has been to try to contain the avian flu by destroying large numbers of poultry that might be carriers of the virus. In the Asian outbreaks, for example, more than 120 million birds died or were destroyed within three months. Fears of the disease and actions taken to halt its spread have hit the Asian economy hard, already causing more than $15 million in losses in the poultry trade. As the National Academy of Science's Institute of Medicine puts it, "[The] current ongoing epidemic of H5N1 avian influenza in Asia is unprecedented in its scale, in its spread, and in the economic losses it has caused."[27]

Despite these efforts to control the spread of H5N1, however, the virus has grown ever stronger and deadlier, killing a widening number of species. In early 2004, the virus developed an ability to kill wild rodents, and it later moved on to domestic pigs that were housed near chickens and also to tigers and leopards that were fed infected poultry in Thailand zoos. The virus apparently adapted so it could survive without a blood supply in chicken feces and the meat of dead chickens.

Health researchers closely watched the progression of the bird flu, worrying that the virus might eventually develop the ability

The Spread of Avian Influenza
Confirmed Cases from 2003 through June 2006

Confirmed Number of Human Cases since 2003

1. Azerbaijan: 8 cases, 5 deaths
2. Cambodia: 6 cases, 6 deaths
3. China: 19 cases, 12 deaths
4. Djibouti: 1 case, 0 deaths
5. Egypt: 14 cases, 6 deaths
6. Indonesia: 49 cases, 37 deaths
7. Iraq: 2 cases, 2 deaths
8. Thailand: 22 cases, 14 deaths
9. Turkey: 12 cases, 4 deaths
10. Vietnam: 93 cases, 42 deaths

H5N1 in wild birds
H5N1 in poultry and wild birds
H5N1 in humans

Sources: U.S. Department of Health & Human Services (www.pandemicflu.gov) and World Health Organization (www.who.int).

to cross the species barrier and infect humans. These fears came true in 1997, when the virus caused infection in eighteen people who worked with poultry in Hong Kong, killing six. As years passed, other isolated bird flu deaths have been confirmed in China and Vietnam. By the end of 2005, close to seventy people had died from the disease worldwide, most of them in Asia. In early 2006, however, fifteen deaths from bird flu were reported in Turkey, the largest number recorded in a bird flu outbreak. In humans, the virus strikes deep in the lungs, making it unusually lethal; the death rate has been over 50 percent.

These human cases have raised the specter of a new, worldwide flu pandemic, perhaps worse than the horrific Spanish flu of 1918. In fact, this avian flu strain is similar to the 1918 flu, causing strikingly similar symptoms. Previously healthy people are suddenly overcome by coughing, headache, high fever, body aches, dizziness, and diarrhea; they soon develop pneumonia, internal bleeding, meningitis, and inability to breathe; and they either recover or die a quick death. With the virus's recent leap from animals to humans, only one prerequisite for a pandemic

remains—the ability for the virus to be easily transmitted between humans. So far, only one isolated case of such human-to-
human transmission has been confirmed, in Thailand in 2004
(although other cases are suspected). If the virus evolves in this
way, everyone in the world will be vulnerable to infection, not
just people who have close contact with poultry and livestock.

The likelihood of such an avian flu pandemic actually hap-
pening, however, is a subject of much debate. On the one hand,
a pandemic is entirely possible if H5N1 becomes capable of
human-to-human transmission and continues to be as contagious and strong in humans as it has been in birds. On the other
hand, scientists can never predict whether or how a particular
virus will mutate, and it is therefore also possible that nothing
will happen. Fears about flu pandemics have proved unfounded
before. As recently as 1976, scientists in the United States similarly warned that a flu pandemic might be on its way after a new
flu strain emerged at a military base in New Jersey. The government swung into action and funded a massive vaccine program,
but the flu pandemic never arrived.

Another consideration is that scientists and doctors now have
many more tools than they did in the past to fight a potential
pandemic. Existing flu vaccines and antiviral drugs might be effective, as well as antibiotics and other drugs to treat flu patients
who develop conditions such as pneumonia or asthma. Drug
companies, too, would immediately begin working to develop a
new vaccine to protect people against a new virus. There is also
now a worldwide public health network that would quickly warn
people of a pandemic threat before it spreads widely, giving many
the chance to avoid exposure. Even if there is a pandemic threat,
therefore, humankind has a good chance of stopping or controlling a disease outbreak before it spreads around the globe.

Costs of the Next Pandemic

If the world does one day face a new flu or other pandemic,
however, the costs and ramifications could well be catastrophic.
U.S. health officials estimate that even a medium-level epidemic
could kill 207,000 Americans, hospitalize 734,000, sicken as
much as one-third of the U.S. population, and translate into

How Viruses Attack

Unlike bacteria, the smallest of which contain five thousand to ten thousand genes, viruses tend to be relatively simple microorganisms, basically a piece of nucleic acid surrounded by a coat of protein molecules. Viruses such as those that cause measles, yellow fever, poliomyelitis, hemorrhagic fever, and HIV, for example, all have fewer than ten genes each. Viruses can multiply only by invading a healthy cell. The virus attaches itself to the surface of a living cell and then penetrates the cell wall by binding its proteins with cell receptors found on the cell's surface. Once inside the cell, the virus moves to the cell nucleus, where it uses the cell's information to replicate its own genes and reproduce. Viruses are also able to "reassort," or mix their genes with those of other viruses present in the host, sometimes forming completely new viral strains. Viruses cause disease either by killing the host cell, altering its function, or affecting the body's immune system in a way that destroys cells and damages vital tissues. Once an animal or person is infected, it either dies or recovers from the infection (often with life-long immunity), or the infection becomes chronic, persisting for years.

This sequence of photographs shows a flu virus penetrating and infecting a human host cell.

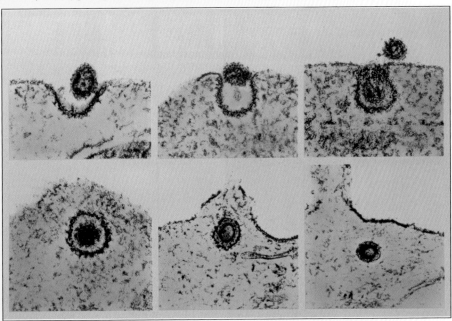

medical costs of more than $166 billion. A more widespread pandemic similar to the 1918 Spanish flu would be even worse. If a deadly flu infection spread as fast as the 1918 flu, U.S. emergency rooms and hospitals would be quickly overwhelmed; people would fail to report to work, crippling government services, utilities, and businesses; and dead bodies would pile up in mortuaries, waiting for burial. In such a flu pandemic, up to 80 million Americans could be infected and, even if such a flu kills only 20 percent of those it hits, deaths could rise to 16 million, with incalculable economic losses.

AN ONGOING BATTLE

"We will never get rid of infectious disease, because no sooner have we wiped out one offender than another bug will mutate to bring new forms of disease."

Pete Moore, science writer. Pete Moore, *Killer Germs: Rogue Diseases of the Twenty-First Century*. London: Carlton Books, 2001, p. 210.

The rest of the developed world would face similar devastation, and less developed countries, where many people's immune systems are already weakened by HIV/AIDS and other infections, would suffer even greater casualties. Globally, the death toll could reach 360 million, more than five times the total number of documented AIDS deaths. With so many people dying all at once in the pandemic, panic would set in and many countries would be overwhelmed, unable to provide health care, maintain security, or keep the economy functioning. These conditions, in turn, could disrupt the world economy, topple stock markets, cause shortages of food and other essential items, create political instability, and cost governments around the world hundreds of billions in lost revenues. Epidemiologist Michael Osterholm warns:

> [If a pandemic began today, national leaders would likely] close most international and even some state or provincial borders. . . . Border security would be made a prior-

ity, especially to protect potential supplies of pandemic-specific vaccines from nearby desperate countries. Military leaders would have to develop strategies to defend the country and also protect against domestic insurgency with armed forces that would likely be compromised by the disease. . . . Even in unaffected countries, fear, panic, and chaos would spread as international media reported the daily advance of the disease around the world. In short order, the global economy would shut down. . . . The labor force would be severely affected when it was most needed. Over the course of the year, up to 50 percent of affected populations could become ill; as many as five percent could die. . . . There would be major shortages in all countries of a wide range of commodities, including food, soap, paper, light bulbs, gasoline, parts for repairing military equipment and municipal water pumps, and medicines, including vaccines unrelated to the pandemic. Many industries not critical to survival—electronics, automobile, and clothing, for example—would suffer or even close. Activities that require close human contact—school, seeing movies in theaters, or eating at restaurants—would be avoided, maybe even banned.[28]

In such a worst-case scenario, the international community would look to the United States, Europe, Japan, and Canada for answers. The developed world would suddenly face an immense burden of caring for its own citizens while also providing vaccines, medicines, and hope for the rest of the world's nations. Depending on how these challenges were handled, and whether poorer nations were provided sufficient aid, the pandemic could also produce political fallout that could affect the path of world history. Given the potentially disastrous consequences of a future pandemic, most health experts recommend that policy makers plan now to prevent and control such losses.

PREVENTING AND CONTROLLING FUTURE PANDEMICS

Beginning in the 1940s, governments and health leaders moved to establish better systems of monitoring disease outbreaks and responding to public health threats. National health agencies were created in the United States and other developed nations, and the United Nations set up its own health organization to coordinate public health work and policy on an international level. However, because the modern world is so connected and pandemics could now spread much more rapidly, most experts emphasize that the fight against future pandemics will have to become even more global—a prospect that raises many practical, financial, and political issues. Despite the challenges ahead, however, there are signs of hope for the future of world health.

Public Health Agencies—CDC and WHO

In the United States, the government agency charged with protecting health and safety is the Centers for Disease Control and Prevention (CDC), part of the U.S. Department of Health and Human Services. Founded in 1946 to help control malaria, the CDC today is the principal U.S. agency involved in efforts to prevent, control, and provide information on all types of medical problems, including infectious disease, chronic disease, workplace and other injuries, disabilities, and environmental health threats.

One branch of the CDC, the National Center for Infectious Diseases (NCID), is dedicated specifically to studying, preventing, and responding to outbreaks of infectious disease. The NCID is often the first responder when a new disease emerges. State as well as international health authorities typically call the NCID for help when faced with a newly emerging infectious agent, and the agency responds by sending a team of disease experts to the location of the outbreak. Once on site, these NCID detectives investigate possible sources of the disease, help to ensure that proper treatment is given to those infected, and educate local residents on the best ways to stop or control the spread of the disease. The NCID team takes samples of the infectious agent and interviews infected people and their family, friends, and other contacts about their actions immediately before

A CDC team unpacks medical equipment and readies itself for an ebola virus investigation in Uganda, Africa.

becoming ill. Clues in the environment, too, such as the presence of wild or domestic animals, insects, or potentially contaminated food and water sources, help team members understand the nature or source of a new disease. CDC's researchers and lab assistants then go to work to identify the germs causing the infection and find cures or vaccines.

BEST EFFORTS

"For mankind to survive [infectious diseases], the best efforts of scientists in medical research are required—not inhibited by political or religious interests, but supported by the full resources of governments and industry with conscientious participation by the general public worldwide."

Michael B.A. Oldstone, immunologist. Michael B.A. Oldstone, *Viruses, Plagues, and History*. New York: Oxford University Press, 1998, p. 157.

On the international level, the main health organization is the World Health Organization (WHO), founded in 1948 by the United Nations, a global political body formed in 1945 by most of the world's countries to promote worldwide peace, security, and economic development. WHO's goal is to help all peoples of the world achieve the best possible state of health, which WHO defines as "complete physical, mental and social well-being and not merely the absence of disease or infirmity."[29] WHO works to coordinate health policies among 192 member nations that make up a body called the World Health Assembly, which votes on WHO's programs and budget.

For countries that have no national health agencies, WHO provides assistance for health-related problems, including emerging diseases. Countries with disease outbreaks contact the organization, and WHO, like the CDC program in the United States, responds with experts and advice. WHO has led the global fight against infectious diseases such as smallpox, malaria, tuberculosis, and HIV/AIDS and works with other health organizations to monitor, track, and predict future disease epidemics. Through education, training, vaccination programs, and health grants, WHO tries to prevent the spread of infectious disease around the world.

Both WHO and the United States have developed pandemic-response plans to prepare for future pandemics. WHO encourages national governments to develop their own plans for handling a pandemic within their borders and promotes coordination and cooperation among nations in order to form a global strategy to control any new infectious disease. So far, however, only about a fifth of the world's countries have prepared a pandemic-response plan, and some of those existing plans are not very comprehensive.

The United States began working on a pandemic plan in 1993, and in the fall of 2005 released a final plan that focuses on preparing for the avian flu. One of the main goals of the U.S. plan is the stockpiling of current flu vaccine and antiviral drugs along with ventilators and other medical equipment necessary for responding to a flu epidemic. Another goal is improving state and local preparedness to contain and manage an outbreak once it occurs. The plan also addresses the need to provide accurate information to the public to avoid panic. Altogether, the plan calls for $7.1 billion worth of funding. Even with full funding, however, U.S. government officials admit that it will take four to five years for the United States to produce enough vaccine to inoculate the 20 million Americans targeted in the plan—that is, less than 10 percent of the U.S. population. Moreover, in December 2005, Congress approved spending only $3.8 billion of the $7.1 billion proposed, providing only part of what authorities believe is necessary to prepare for the bird flu. Some lawmakers plan to push for more funds to be authorized in 2006.

The Need for a Global Response

The efforts of national governments are important, but health experts say that the real key to preparing for the next pandemic is a strong global approach. Despite WHO's efforts to promote cooperation among nations, in today's health care system each country is concerned mostly with looking after its own interests and using its sometimes limited resources to benefit only its own citizens. According to health authorities, a truly global

Poverty and Infectious Disease

The scourge of HIV/AIDS, TB, and malaria infections in undeveloped countries, health experts say, demonstrates the link between poverty and infectious disease. Most people in developed countries like the United States live in relative affluence, but in much of the world, one in five people live in poverty. These millions of poor people struggle daily with conditions such as malnourishment, contaminated drinking water, untreated sewage, and filthy, substandard housing. Many children do not attend school or receive health care, vaccinations, or sex education. Doctors and health clinics are often not available or are located too far away to allow sick people to receive proper medical attention. Roads are often impassable, preventing health workers from traveling to remote villages. These conditions produce disease, encourage the spread of infections, and impede proper treatment. As global health expert Bill Foege explains, "When a child dies in West Africa, it in no way depicts the truth that that child was malnourished, that child also had malaria, probably had schistosomiasis and onchocerciasis and lymphatic filariasis [infections by parasitic worms] and hookworms and roundworms. All of those things together allowed measles to be the final assault."

Bill Foege, quoted in Madeline Drexler, *Secret Agents: The Menace of Emerging Infections.* Washington, DC: Joseph Henry, 2002, p. 283.

approach that distributes resources efficiently to the most important areas and focuses on stopping outbreaks at their source would be much more effective—for all countries. After all, once infectious disease breaks out, it can spread swiftly to other nations no matter how officials try to stop it by closing borders or taking other restrictive actions. As journalist Madeline Drexler puts it, "There are no national borders against infection."[30]

Such a global health system would provide for better worldwide monitoring and tracking of new types of infectious agents and an aggressive, multinational response to investigate, identify, and contain new diseases no matter where new outbreaks occur. Such a system would require more disease observation posts, more laboratories that are properly equipped and staffed to rapidly test new pathogens, and better communication networks to alert governments and health departments around the world quickly and freely about disease outbreaks. Once outbreaks occur, each country must be aided to manage the crisis within its borders, consistent with international health policies.

Building a global health system, experts say, requires political will and commitment and a recognition by all national governments that a disease outbreak in one country is truly a threat to the entire world. Most important is providing funding to developing countries to enable them to build the monitoring facilities and labs, hire the trained personnel, and purchase the medical equipment, vaccines, and drugs necessary to respond to a pandemic. Dr. David Nabarro, the United Nations' senior coordinator for avian and human influenza, explains:

> If [a pandemic] starts spreading among people . . . we will have very little time to respond. The first things

Sudanese villagers carry a patient on a stretcher to a waiting ambulance so she can see a doctor.

we'll need are good surveillance systems and fast, open communications. We know from the SARS epidemic that you can't have an effective response unless governments share information quickly and freely, and in ways that keep people from panicking. Panic can set off migrations that affect everything from air travel to housing and food supplies. The other priority is to quickly isolate affected people and their contacts. You've got to have [drugs] on hand to treat people at risk of exposure, and you've got to have masks and protective clothing available to health workers. That's a lot to ask of countries that lack functioning health systems. Can they afford to invest for potential health problems when they're so burdened by real ones? We can't put the burden on individual countries. This is a global danger, and we need a global framework for responding to it.[31]

Preparing for the Avian Flu

The prospect of an avian flu pandemic has raised another difficult problem—producing enough vaccines to immunize large numbers of people around the world and enough antiflu drugs to control the severity of disease in the millions who will likely become infected. In recent years, the world's vaccine-producing capacity has substantially declined because the vaccine market is both risky and unprofitable. Flu viruses change quickly and often, so companies must produce a different vaccine each year and take the risk that there will be a market for it. If a flu season is mild, sales and profits are low, and the remaining vaccine cannot be sold the following year. Today, despite the dire warnings from health officials about a coming pandemic, only nine countries have companies that are working to produce an avian flu vaccine—Australia, Britain, Canada, France, Germany, Italy, Japan, the Netherlands, and the United States. Indeed, Debora Mackenzie and Kristin Choo, reporters for the magazine *New Scientist*, explain, "Nearly 70 per cent of the world's vaccine manufacturing capacity is in five countries in western Europe."[32]

Experts predict that the countries with vaccine production capacity may be reluctant to export vaccine in the event of a

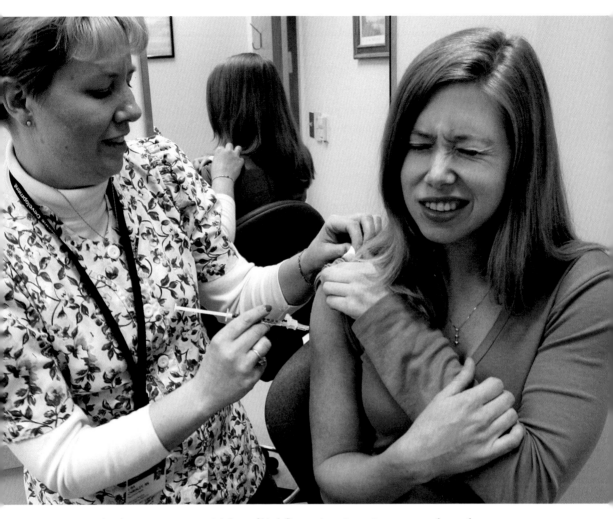

A volunteer accepts a trial dose of bird-flu vaccine. A vaccine may soon be ready, but there may not be enough for all who need it.

pandemic, at least until their own populations are immunized—a prospect that could leave many other countries at the mercy of a lethal flu virus. Poorer, less developed countries, for example, have no vaccine producers and, even if they had the funds to purchase vaccines or drugs, would be entirely dependent on obtaining vaccine from foreign countries. Even the United States, the world's most affluent country, might find itself without enough flu vaccine. Most U.S. drug companies have largely abandoned the vaccine market because it is so unprofitable, and the United States now relies on only four companies—Sanofi Pasteur Inc., MedImmune Vaccines Inc., Chiron Corporation, and GlaxoSmithKline Inc.—for its annual vaccine supply. Recently, these companies have failed to produce enough flu vaccine even during normal flu seasons, leaving Americans dependent on foreign vaccine suppliers and at great risk should a flu pandemic arise.

AVIAN FLU TRAGEDY

"Millions will not receive [avian flu] vaccine, and thousands will die. Economists call this an opportunity cost. I call it a tragedy."

David Fedson, founder of the vaccine industry's pandemic task force. Quoted in Debora Mackenzie and Kristin Choo, "Bird Flu: Kick-start Vaccination or Face the Consequences: The World Needs a Global Action Plan, and Fast, If We Are to Stand Any Hope of Stopping a Flu Pandemic," *New Scientist*, October 15, 2005, p. 6.

The result is that, although researchers have already developed a vaccine that may be effective against the H5N1 bird flu virus, there simply are not enough manufacturers to produce the vaccine in the quantities that would be needed for a pandemic. Existing manufacturers can make only about 900 million doses of vaccine over a normal six-month production cycle. This may sound like a lot, but scientists warn that because H5N1 is new to people's immune systems, each person would probably need two vaccinations a few weeks apart, in dosages much higher than those for typical flu vaccines. Current production levels would thus supply only enough vaccine to immunize about 75 million people, roughly one quarter of the U.S. population. Only now are companies beginning to test ways to stretch the vaccine to cover more people. One promising method is to combine the vaccine with an immunity-boosting chemical called an adjuvant. Even if this method is successful in producing a low-dose vaccine, however, the best scenario is that enough hybrid vaccine might be produced to protect only about 3.5 billion people, far less than the worldwide population of 6.5 billion.

If a sufficient supply of hybrid vaccine is not available and a pandemic hits, vaccine rationing would thus be necessary. Rationing, however, raises difficult questions about equitable distribution, both between competing countries and within each country's population. Would only rich, powerful countries like the United States get the vaccine, or would developing countries also get their fair share? Within the United States, would vaccine be reserved for critical health care workers, politicians, and other designated occupations? Would at-risk groups such as the elderly, the very young, and pregnant women receive priority? How would class, race, and wealth affect people's access to vaccine? The solution, experts say, is a global program to speed up vaccine production as soon as possible. Pandemic expert Michael Osterholm urges, "An initiative to provide vaccine for the entire world must be developed, with a well-defined schedule to ensure progress. . . . Pandemic-influenza preparedness is by nature an international issue. No one can truly be isolated from a pandemic."[33]

Of course, there is also a possibility that the avian flu virus will mutate in ways that would make the hybrid vaccine ineffective. If this happens, scientists will be forced to develop a

Gene Therapy

Scientists believe that gene therapy—the introduction of new genetic material into human cells to cure or control disease—holds great potential for the treatment of infectious diseases. One approach is to introduce genes into the body that will block or inhibit the reproduction or spread of infectious viruses at the cellular or other levels. Genes also might be used to stimulate the body's production of certain proteins or immune responses that will fight viral or bacterial infection. Today, researchers are investigating gene therapy as a possible treatment for many infectious diseases, including the HIV virus that causes AIDS. Dr. Gary Nabel of the University of Michigan Medical Center, for example, has devised a method of modifying T cells, which are part of the body's immune system, to fight HIV. Nabel extracted the T cells from HIV-infected patients and inserted into them an HIV gene that inhibits replication of the virus. When they were injected back into patients, the modified T cells were able to survive much longer than regular T cells. Scientists hope that, one day, they will be able to use gene therapy to fight or even cure AIDS and other lethal infectious diseases.

A Taiwanese official unpacks boxes of the avian-flu drug Tamiflu, adding to the government's stockpile.

new vaccine specific to the strain of flu that is causing the pandemic. This research process, however, may take months, with many more months devoted to producing an adequate supply of the new vaccine and distributing it around the world. By then, the avian flu may have time to spread widely, negating the usefulness of a preventive vaccine.

Yet another approach to fighting an avian flu pandemic would be the use of antiviral drugs that, if given early when symptoms first appear, can help infected patients fight off flu viruses. One such drug, oseltamivir (called Tamiflu) is expected to be effective in cases of bird flu. As a result, one of the main strategies for preparing for a possible flu pandemic is to create stockpiles of Tamiflu around the world. This drug, however, is in short supply because it is manufactured by only one company—Roche Pharmaceuticals—in a single plant in Switzerland. Many poor countries cannot afford to stock up on Tamiflu because they are struggling to deal with other health crises, such as HIV/AIDS. In addition, there are signs that the bird flu may be developing a resistance to Tamiflu. In 2005, two patients in Vietnam infected with a particular strain of H5N1 died after failing to respond to treatment with Tamiflu. If antivirals do not work in an avian flu pandemic, the world's defenses will be severely crippled.

Similar problems of scarcity or ineffectiveness of existing drugs may arise if another pathogen sparks the next pandemic. With the rise of many types of bacteria that are resistant to today's panoply of antibiotic drugs, the next pandemic may come from a bacterial rather than a viral source, raising the specter of a new plague that has no effective cure. Health experts are worried because many large drug companies have dropped or significantly cut back on their antibiotic research programs, reducing the numbers of new antibiotic drugs available to doctors. Between 1998 and 2003, for example, only nine new antibiotics were approved. With health experts cautioning against the overuse of antibiotics, many companies apparently fear a declining market. The U.S. government, therefore, is trying to encourage the drug companies to again embrace antibiotic research. By providing incentives such as speeding up the Food and Drug Administration process for approving new drugs, changing requirements to allow for smaller clinical testing of such drugs, and giving manufacturers longer periods to sell the new drug without competition from other companies, the government hopes to jump-start this area of research.

Reasons for Hope

Despite the seemingly gloomy state of global health and the fears of a new disease pandemic, many health experts are more optimistic than ever before about the prospects for improving health around the world. Today, as never before, philanthropists, governments, and private industry are awakening to the need for cooperation on health problems and are funding international health initiatives aimed at defeating the suffering caused by poverty, infection, and disease. At long last, people may be realizing that in a globalized world, no one country is safe from disease until all have adequate health care. Dr. Gro Harlem Brundtland, director-general of WHO, states, "The landscape for international health has changed dramatically."[34]

A LACK OF WILL?

"It's an amazing thing to think that ours is the first generation in history that really can end extreme poverty, the kind that means a child dies for lack of food in its belly. . . . We have the science, the technology, and the wealth. What we don't have is the will, and that's not a reason that history will accept."

Bono, rock singer and social activist. Quoted in World Association Newspapers, Bono Interview, "Death Statistics Brought to Life," May 4, 2004. www.news24.com/News24/World/PressFreedomDay/ 0,,2-10-1604_1520175,00.html.

This phenomenon began just in the last few years, when several private individuals donated or organized donations of huge sums of money to projects aimed at improving international health. One of these influential new philanthropists is Paul David Hewson, known as Bono, the lead singer in the Irish rock band U2. Since 1999, Bono has become increasingly involved in campaigns to help Africa fight HIV/AIDS and other pandemic diseases. In 2002, Bono set up an organization called DATA, which is short for Debt, AIDS, Trade, Africa, to raise awareness about AIDS and other problems facing the region. Bono has focused on pressuring governments to forgive debt and increase their foreign aid to developing countries. In 2005, thanks to Bono's efforts, the world's richest countries forgave $40 billion in debt owed by the poorest, allowing them to spend precious resources on health care instead. In January 2006, Bono launched a new partnership with American Express and other companies aimed at producing funds that will be given to the Global Fund to Fight AIDS, Tuberculosis and Malaria, the international organization devoted to these global health issues.

An even bigger private player in the forefront of today's battle against infectious disease is the Bill and Melinda Gates Foundation, a private charitable organization created and endowed

Time *magazine honored Bill Gates, Bono, and Melinda Gates for their impressive contributions to global health campaigns.*

by Bill Gates, the founder of Microsoft, the world's leading computer software company. Since it was funded with an initial $5 billion in 1999, the foundation has poured billions of dollars into global health. In 2000, for example, the fund spent over $1 billion on health projects. Since 2001, it has pledged $150 million to the Global Fund to Fight AIDS, Tuberculosis and Malaria. In 2002, the foundation donated more than $100 million to help children suffering from AIDS in India. In 2005, the foundation donated a massive $750 million to launch the Global Alliance for Vaccines and Immunizations, a coalition of international public health agencies, philanthropists, and drug companies, whose mission is to develop and deliver vaccines for various diseases, including HIV, tuberculosis, and malaria. Today, following a recent gift from investment guru Warren Buffet, the Gates foundation has an endowment of more than $60

Diligent research and generous monetary investments can help control current pandemics and maybe also prevent future ones.

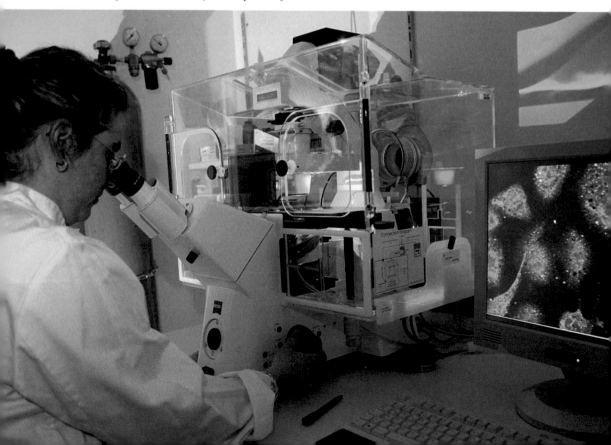

billion and is expected to donate at least $1 billion each year to global health causes. In recognition of their tremendous impact in the health care field, *Time* magazine named Bill and Melinda Gates, along with Bono, "persons of the year" for 2005.

The work of these and other individuals has raised awareness about global health issues and may be stimulating greater government and corporate responsibility in health matters. In 2001, for example, several of the world's major drug companies, in response to enormous public pressure, dropped a lawsuit challenging South Africa's right to import cheap, generic versions of AIDS drugs. In 2005 and 2006, Roche, the maker of Tamiflu, donated 5 million doses of the drug to WHO to help build a rapid response stockpile to be used in developing countries in an outbreak of pandemic flu. Meanwhile, the United States has increased its health funding in recent years, both for current pandemic diseases such as HIV/AIDS, TB, and malaria and for future pandemic preparations. The threat of bioterrorism, too, has spurred many governments to fund new research programs focusing on infectious disease and has led to the development of vaccines for ricin and pneumonic plague. In January 2006, countries from around the world met in Beijing, China, and pledged $1.9 billion to support the global campaign against the avian flu. The United States made the largest donation—$334 million. Much of this money will go to less developed countries in the form of grants, to assist them in preparing for an avian flu pandemic.

Many people hope that this new focus on global health—by individuals, corporations, and governments—will help rid the world of today's pandemic diseases and better prepare it to face future pandemic threats. As the Center for Global Development, a private research group, states, "Global health challenges, which are often perceived as daunting, are indeed solvable."[35]

NOTES

Chapter 1: The Threat from Infectious Pandemics

1. Quoted in Arno Karlen, *Man and Microbes*. New York: G.P. Putnam's Sons, 1995, p. 117.

2. Verity Murphy, "Past Pandemics That Ravaged Europe," BBC News, November 7, 2005. http://news.bbc.co.uk/1/hi/health/4381924.stm.

3. Quoted in Pete Moore, *Killer Germs: Rogue Diseases of the Twenty-First Century*. London: Carlton Books, 2001, p. 31.

4. Quoted in Karlen, *Man and Microbes*, p. 102.

5. Molly Billings, "The Influenza Pandemic of 1918," June 1997. www.stanford.edu/group/virus/uda/.

6. Quoted in Laurie Garrett, *The Coming Plague: Newly Emerging Diseases in a World Out of Balance*. New York: Farrar, Straus and Giroux, 1994, p. 47.

7. Quoted in *Pfizer Journal*, "Perils in the Promise of the Antibiotic Era," vol. 5, no. 2, 2004. www.thepfizerjournal.com/default.asp?a=article&j=tpj38&t=Perils%;20in%;20the%;20Promise%;20of%;20the%;20Antibiotic%;20Era.

Chapter 2: The Battle Against Infectious Disease Continues

8. Quoted in *Pfizer Journal*, "Staying Ahead in the Germ Wars," vol. 5, no. 2, 2004. www.thepfizerjournal.com/default.asp?a=article&j=tpj38&t=Staying%;20Ahead%;20In%;20The%;20Germ%;20Wars.

9. David Suzuki, "Human Activities Give Rise to New Diseases," David Suzuki Foundation, May 30, 2003. www.davidsuzuki.org/about_us/Dr_David_Suzuki/Article_Archives/weekly05300301.asp.

10. Quoted in Garrett, *Coming Plague,* p. 431.

11. Quoted in Ricki Lewis, "The Rise of Antibiotic-Resistant Infections," U.S. Food and Drug Administration, *FDA Consumer Magazine*, September 1995. www.fda.gov/fdac/features/795_antibio.html.

12. Quoted in Mathew Gandy and Alimuddin Zumla, eds., *The Return of the White Plague*. New York: Verso, 2003, p. 10.

13. Madeline Drexler, *Secret Agents: The Menace of Emerging Infections*. Washington, DC: Joseph Henry, 2002, pp. 132–33.

Chapter 3: Fighting Today's Pandemics

14. Quoted in John Christensen, "AIDS in Africa: Dying by the Numbers," CNN, 2001. www.cnn.com/SPECIALS/2000/aids/stories/overview/.

15. Greg Behrman, *The Invisible People: How the U.S. Has Slept Through the Global AIDS Pandemic: The Greatest Humanitarian Catastrophe of Our Time*. New York: Free Press, 2004, p. xiii.

16. Lawrence O. Gostin, *The AIDS Pandemic*. Chapel Hill: University of North Carolina Press, 2004, p. xxix.

17. Gostin, *AIDS Pandemic*, p. 318.

18. Gandy and Zumla, *Return of the White Plague*, p. 237.

19. *Boston Globe*, "AIDS Disaster Relief," October 18, 2005. www.boston.com/news/globe/editorial_opinion/editorials/articles/2005/10/18/aids_disaster_relief/.

20. Alfred J. Bollett, *Plagues and Poxes: The Impact of Human History on Epidemic Disease*. New York: Demos Medical Publishing, 2004, p. 221.

21. Michael B.A. Oldstone, *Viruses, Plagues, and History*. New York: Oxford University Press, 1998, p. 119.

Chapter 4: Future Pandemic Threats

22. Drexler, *Secret Agents*, pp. 231–32.

23. Quoted in PBS, *Frontline*, "Plague War: Interview, Michael Osterholm," 1998. www.pbs.org/wgbh/pages/frontline/shows/plague/interviews/osterholm.html.

24. Quoted in *Nature*, "The 1918 Flu Virus Is Resurrected," October 6, 2005, pp. 794–95.

25. Quoted in *Nature*, "The 1918 Flu Virus Is Resurrected."

26. Debora Mackenzie, "Lab Slip-Up Could Trigger Next Flu Pandemic," *New Scientist*, April 23, 2005, p. 11.

27. Quoted in Laurie Garrett, "The Next Pandemic?" *Foreign Affairs*, July–August 2005, p. 3.

28. Michael T. Osterholm, "Preparing for the Next Pandemic," *Foreign Affairs*, July–August 2005, p. 4.

Chapter 5: Preventing and Controlling Future Pandemics

29. World Health Organization, "About WHO," 2006. www.who.int/about/en/.

30. Drexler, *Secret Agents*, p. 282.

31. Quoted in Geoffrey Cowley, "Bracing for a Plague: The Physician Charged with Preparing the World for a Flu Pandemic Reflects on the Threat," *Newsweek*, December 12, 2005, p. 72.

32. Debora Mackenzie and Kristin Choo, "Bird Flu: Kick-start Vaccination or Face the Consequences: The World Needs a Global Action Plan, and Fast, If We Are to Stand Any Hope of Stopping a Flu Pandemic," *New Scientist*, October 15, 2005, p. 6.

33. Osterholm, "Preparing for the Next Pandemic," p. 4.

34. Quoted in Drexler, *Secret Agents*, p. 286.

35. Center for Global Development, "Millions Saved: Proven Successes in Global Health," 2006. www.cgdev.org/section/initiatives/_active/millionssaved/.

DISCUSSION QUESTIONS

Chapter 1: The Threat from Infectious Pandemics

1. According to the author, how did infectious diseases affect the history of the Americas?

2. Which past pandemic killed the greatest number of people? Which was the most deadly in a short period of time?

3. Name some of the scientific heroes who helped the world fight infectious disease in the late 1800s and early 1900s, and describe their contributions.

Chapter 2: The Battle Against Infectious Disease Continues

1. What are some of the factors that, according to the book, are contributing to the rise of infectious disease today?

2. How is HIV/AIDS spread?

3. Besides the three top disease threats—AIDS, tuberculosis, and malaria—what other infectious diseases are on the rise today?

Chapter 3: Fighting Today's Pandemics

1. According to the author, what regions of the world have the highest incidence of HIV/AIDS infection today?

2. How does the book explain the spread of tuberculosis and malaria, since they are usually curable, preventable illnesses?

3. What lesson in disease control did the world learn from the SARS epidemic?

Chapter 4: Future Pandemic Threats

1. What makes viruses and bacteria effective as possible weapons of mass destruction, according to sources quoted by the author?

2. What is the status of the avian flu virus, and what development is required before the virus could spread to become a pandemic threat?

3. Is an avian flu pandemic certain to happen? How are science and medicine different today from the days of the 1918 Spanish flu pandemic?

Chapter 5: Preventing and Controlling Future Pandemics

1. What are the names and functions of the main U.S. and international health agencies?

2. According to the book, what are the main obstacles to protecting the world from an avian flu pandemic?

3. Who are the world's biggest private supporters of improvements in global health?

National Center for Infectious Disease (NCID)
Centers for Disease Control and Prevention (CDC)
Milstop C-14, 1600 Clifton Rd., Atlanta, GA 30333
www.cdc.gov/ncidod/

The National Center for Infectious Disease is the United States' main agency involved in the study, prevention, and control of infectious disease. The Web site contains a wealth of information about all types of infectious diseases, as well as links to a government magazine on infectious diseases, with up-to-date articles on various topics.

Pandemicflu.gov
U.S. Department of Health and Human Services (HHS)
200 Independence Ave., SW, Washington, DC 20201
(800) 232-4636
www.pandemicflu.gov/vaccine

This is the U.S. government's official Web site for information on pandemic flu and avian influenza. It is sponsored by the Department of Health and Human Services, the government's principal agency for protecting the health of all Americans. The Web site includes an overview of the avian flu phenomenon, describes U.S. efforts to prepare for a possible pandemic, and provides links to many other Web sites on the subject.

U.S. Agency for International Development (USAID)
Information Center, Ronald Reagan Building,
Washington, DC 20523-1000
(202) 712-4810
www.usaid.gov/index.html

The U.S. Agency for International Development is the principal U.S. agency that provides assistance to countries recovering from disaster, trying to escape poverty, and engaging in democratic reforms. Its goal is to advance U.S. foreign policy objectives by supporting initiatives for global health, economic growth, humanitarian assistance, and democracy in Africa, Asia, Latin America, and Europe. The USAID Web site provides information about U.S. contributions to global health, including efforts to fight HIV/AIDS and other infectious diseases.

World Health Organization (WHO)
Avenue Appia 20, 1211 Geneva 27, Switzerland
(+ 41 22) 791 21 11
www.who.int/en/

The World Health Organization is the United Nations' specialized agency for health. Its Web site provides a wealth of information and publications about avian flu and many other global health topics, as well as updates on breaking news and global health funding and policies.

FOR MORE INFORMATION

Books

John M. Barry, *The Great Influenza: The Epic Story of the Greatest Plague in History*. New York: Viking, 2004. An entertaining narrative of the 1918 flu pandemic, the fear and panic that accompanied it, and the world's response.

Alfred J. Bollet, *Plagues and Poxes: The Impact of Human History on Epidemic Disease*. New York: Demos Medical Publishing, 2004. A series of essays about disease patterns throughout history and the ways in which human activities have influenced the rise and fall of both infectious and noninfectious disease.

Mark P. Friedlander, *Outbreak: Disease Detectives at Work*. Minneapolis: Lerner, 2003. A young adult selection that describes the field of epidemiology and its history, including historical and modern case studies as well as explanations of various diseases and bioterrorist weapons.

Julie Kramer, *Plague and Pandemic Alert!* New York: Crabtree, 2005. A young adult book about what causes a plague, what a pandemic is, and how they both can be contained or prevented.

Rob LaSalle, *Epidemic!* New York: New Press, 1999. This book for general readers explores the topic of infectious diseases with essays by Nobel Prize–winning experts, profiles of scientists and researchers, case studies, photos, and illustrations.

Michael B.A. Oldstone, *Viruses, Plagues, and History*. New York: Oxford University Press, 1998, p. 157. A readable history of the ways that viruses have affected the history of human civilization.

Stephanie True Peters, *The 1918 Influenza Pandemic*. New York: Benchmark Books, 2005. An exploration of the history and results of the 1918 Spanish influenza pandemic, geared to young adults.

Periodicals

John Carey, Amy Barrett, Nanette Byrnes, and Rachel Tiplady, "Avian Flu: Business Thinks the Unthinkable," *Business Week*, November 28, 2005.

Geoffrey Cowley, "Bracing for a Plague: The Physician Charged with Preparing the World for a Flu Pandemic Reflects on the Threat," *Newsweek*, December 12, 2005.

Nancy Gibbs, "Persons of the Year," *Time*, December 26, 2005.

Christine Gorman, "How Scared Should We Be? Scared Enough to Take Action. Haunted by Katrina, Washington Scrambles to Prepare for a Much Deadlier Kind of Natural Disaster," *Time*, October 17, 2005.

Debora Mackenzie, "Can Tamiflu Save Us From Bird Flu?" *New Scientist*, June 4, 2005.

Wendy Orent, "Chicken Little—We'll Survive the Bird Flu," *New Republic*, September 12, 2005.

Nancy Shute, "Germs on the Loose," *U.S. News & World Report*, April 25, 2005.

Web Sites

ABC News, "Flu" (http://abcnews.go.com/Health/Flu/?CMP= yahoo_health). A media Web site on the avian flu that provides links to the latest news stories and other useful reports and articles.

BBC, "Bird Flu" (http://news.bbc.co.uk/1/hi/in_depth/world/ 2005/bird_flu/default.stm). A British news Web site with news, articles, charts, and videos about the avian flu.

Molly Billings, "The Influenza Pandemic of 1918," June 1997 (www.stanford.edu/group/virus/uda). An entertaining and educational Web site about the 1918 Spanish flu pandemic.

Council on Foreign Relations, "The Next Pandemic?" (www.foreignaffairs.org/background/pandemic). A very informative Web site for a special July–August 2005 issue of *Foreign Affairs* magazine, offering a selection of articles from global health experts about the avian flu, HIV/AIDS, and other topics relevant to global health.

INDEX

PICTURE CREDITS

Cover: © Gideon Mendel/ CORBIS
AFP/Getty Images, 27, 29
AP/Wide World Photos, 9, 48, 57, 64, 75, 79, 84
© Bettmann/CORBIS, 18, 24 (main)
© Dr. Steve Patterson/Photo Researchers, Inc., 71
© Friso Gentsch/DPA/CORBIS, 88
© Geoff Tompkinson/Photo Researcher, Inc., 24 (inset)
Getty Images, 59, 81
Hulton Archive/Getty Images, 19
© Jean-Loup Charmet/Photo Researchers, Inc., 14
© Kent Wood/Photo Researchers, Inc., 7
Kyodo/Landov, 62
Mapping Specialists, 43, 49, 51, 68
Newhouse News Service/Landov, 35
Paul Faith/Empics/Landov, 39
Public Health Image Library, Centers for Disease Control,
    12, 65
Reuters/Frederic J. Brown/Pool/Landov, 33
Roger Viollet/Getty Images, 22
© Science Photo Library/Photo Researchers, Inc., 31
Time & Life Pictures/Getty Images, 45, 87

ABOUT THE AUTHOR

Debra A. Miller is a writer and lawyer with a passion for current events and history. She began her law career in Washington, D.C., where she worked on legislative, policy, and legal matters in government, public interest, and private law firm positions. She now lives with her husband in Encinitas, California, where she writes and edits books and anthologies on historical, political, and other topics.